# Bereavement

Editor: Danielle Lobban

Volume 407

independence
educational publishers

First published by Independence Educational Publishers

The Studio, High Green

Great Shelford

Cambridge CB22 5EG

England

## Copyright

## Photocopy licence

ISBN-13: 978 1 86168 866 8

## Printed in Great Britain

Zenith Print Group

# Contents

# Introduction

**Bereavement** is Volume 407 in the **issues** series. The aim of the series is to offer current, diverse information about important issues in our world, from a UK perspective.

## About Bereavement

The loss of a loved one can be one of the most difficult times in your life. This book explores how grief can affect us, as well as ways to cope and how to support those who have experienced loss. It also looks at issues that surround death such as funeral planning and creating a will.

## OUR SOURCES

Titles in the **issues** series are designed to function as educational resource books, providing a balanced overview of a specific subject.

The information in our books is comprised of facts, articles and opinions from many different sources, including:

♦ Newspaper reports and opinion pieces

♦ Website factsheets

♦ Magazine and journal articles

♦ Statistics and surveys

♦ Government reports

♦ Literature from special interest groups.

## A NOTE ON CRITICAL EVALUATION

Because the information reprinted here is from a number of different sources, readers should bear in mind the origin of the text and whether the source is likely to have a particular bias when presenting information (or when conducting their research). It is hoped that, as you read about the many aspects of the issues explored in this book, you will critically evaluate the information presented.

It is important that you decide whether you are being presented with facts or opinions. Does the writer give a biased or unbiased report? If an opinion is being expressed, do you agree with the writer? Is there potential bias to the 'facts' or statistics behind an article?

## ASSIGNMENTS

In the back of this book, you will find a selection of assignments designed to help you engage with the articles you have been reading and to explore your own opinions. Some tasks will take longer than others and there is a mixture of design, writing and research-based activities that you can complete alone or in a group.

## FURTHER RESEARCH

At the end of each article we have listed its source and a website that you can visit if you would like to conduct your own research. Please remember to critically evaluate any sources that you consult and consider whether the information you are viewing is accurate and unbiased.

# Useful Websites

www.ataloss.org

www.beyond.life

www.counselling-directory.org.uk

www.countrynavigator.com

www.cruse.org.uk

www.help2makesense.org

www.hopeagain.org.uk

www.hospiceuk.org

www.humanists.uk

www.independent.co.uk

www.metro.co.uk

www.mind.org.uk

www.skillsyouneed.com

www.sueryder.org

www.theconversation.com

www.thegazette.co.uk

www.verywellhealth.com

www.yougov.co.uk

# What physically happens to your body right after death

From the moment of death to rigor mortis and beyond.

## By Chris Raymond

It is difficult to generalize how people will respond to the subject of death because each of us is different. But, generally speaking, people feel uncomfortable at the thought of their own mortality.

What often underlies this uneasiness is the actual process of dying (and the fear of a prolonged or painful death) rather than the state of being dead. Few people seem to wonder what actually happens to the body after you die.

Here is a timeline of the changes the body undergoes immediately following death. This article walks you through the processes from the moment a person dies right through the various post-mortem (post-death) stages.

### At the moment of death

We often think of the moment of death as that time at which the heartbeat and breathing stop. We are learning, however, that death isn't instantaneous. Our brains are now thought to continue to 'work' for 10 minutes or so after we die, meaning that our brains may, in some way, be aware of our death.

In the hospital setting, there are a few criteria doctors use to declare death. These include the absence of a pulse, the absence of breathing, the absence of reflexes, and the absence of pupil contraction to bright light.

In an emergency setting, paramedics look for the five signs of irreversible death to determine when resuscitation, or revival, is not possible.

By definition, death is either when circulatory and respiratory functions stop irreversibly, or brain death, when the entire brain, including the brainstem, stop functioning. The determination must be made according to accepted medical standards.

### Recap

Death is declared either when there is brain death (no function of the entire brain and brainstem) or breathing and circulation cannot be restored with resuscitation efforts.

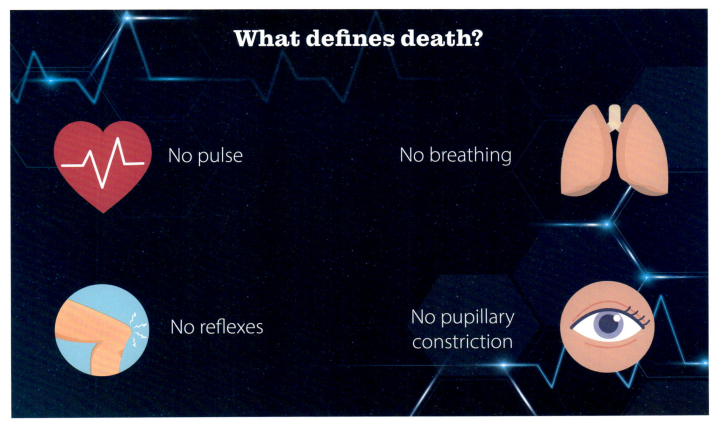

**What defines death?**

No pulse

No breathing

No reflexes

No pupillary constriction

## At hour 1

At the moment of death, all of the muscles in the body relax, a state called primary flaccidity. Eyelids lose their tension, the pupils dilate, the jaw might fall open, and the body's joints and limbs are flexible.

With the loss of tension in the muscles, the skin will sag, which can cause prominent joints and bones in the body, such as the jaw or hips, to become pronounced. As muscles relax, sphincters release and allow urine and faeces to pass.

Within minutes of the heart stopping, a process called pallor mortis causes the body to grow pale as the blood drains from the smaller veins in the skin. This process may be more visible in those with light skin rather than darker skin.

The human heart beats more than 2.5 billion times during the average human lifespan, circulating about 5.6 litres (6 quarts) of blood through the circulatory system.

At the same time, the body begins to cool from its normal temperature of 98.6 F (37 C) until reaching the air temperature around it. Known as algor mortis or the 'death chill,' body temperature falls at a somewhat steady rate of 1.5 degrees F per hour.

The expected decrease in body temperature during algor mortis can help forensic scientists approximate the time of death, assuming the body hasn't completely cooled or been exposed to extreme environmental temperatures.

### Recap

At the time of death, all of the muscles of the body will relax, called primary flaccidity. This will be followed within minutes by a visible paling of the skin, called pallor mortis.

## At hours 2 to 6

Because the heart no longer pumps blood, gravity begins to pull it to the areas of the body closest to the ground (pooling), a process called livor mortis.

If the body remains undisturbed for several hours, the parts of the body nearest the ground can develop a reddish-purple discolouration resembling a bruise caused by the accumulation of blood. Embalmers sometimes refer to this as the 'postmortem stain.'

Beginning approximately in the third hour after death, chemical changes within the body's cells cause all of the muscles to begin stiffening, known as rigor mortis. With rigor mortis, the first muscles affected will be the eyelids, jaw, and neck.

Over the next several hours, rigor mortis will spread into the face and down through the chest, abdomen, arms, and legs until it finally reaches the fingers and toes.

Interestingly, the old custom of placing coins on the eyelids of the deceased might have originated from the desire to keep the eyes shut since rigor mortis affects them soonest. Also, it is not unusual for infants and young children who die to not display rigor mortis, possibly due to their smaller muscle mass.

### Recap

Rigor mortis, the stiffening of muscles following death, usually starts three hours after a person dies. The stiffening starts around the head and neck and gradually progresses downward toward the feet and toes.

## At hours 7 to 12

Maximum muscle stiffness throughout the body occurs after roughly 12 hours due to rigor mortis, although this will be affected by the person's age, physical condition, gender, the air temperature, and other factors.

At this point, the limbs of the deceased are difficult to move or manipulate. The knees and elbows will be slightly flexed, and fingers or toes can appear unusually crooked.

## From Hour 12 and Beyond

After reaching a state of maximum rigor mortis, the muscles will begin to loosen due to continued chemical changes within the cells and internal tissue decay. The process, known as secondary flaccidity, occurs over a period of one to three days and is affected by external conditions such as temperature. Cold slows down the process.

During secondary flaccidity, the skin will begin to shrink, creating the illusion that hair and nails are growing. Rigor mortis will then dissipate in the opposite direction–from the fingers and toes to the face–over a period of up to 48 hours.

Once secondary flaccidity is complete, all of the muscles of the body will again be relaxed.

### Recap

Rigor mortis is usually complete 12 hours after death. Thereafter, the muscles will start to relax over the course of one to three days in a process called secondary flaccidity.

## Summary

Death is declared when there is either brain death or all efforts to resuscitate a person have failed. From the moment of death, physical changes will start to take place:

♦ Within one hour: Primary flaccidity (relaxation of muscles) will occur almost immediately followed by pallor mortis (paling of the skin).

♦ At two to six hours: Rigor mortis (stiffening of muscles) will begin.

♦ At seven to 12 hours: Rigor mortis is complete.

♦ From 12 hours: Secondary flaccidity will start and be completed within one to three days.

### A Word From Verywell

Some people do not want to think about the changes in the body after death, whereas others wish to know. Everyone is different, and it is a very personal decision.

For those who wish to know, however, we are learning that the bodily changes leading up to death, and after death, aren't simply random decomposition. Our bodies are actually designed to shut down and die at some time in a programmed manner

*8 December 2021*

## Frequently asked questions

### What happens to a person's body right after they die?

Immediately, all muscles relax and the body becomes limp. The sphincters also relax and the body releases urine and faeces. Skin tone also becomes pale and body temperature begins to drop.

### What part of your body dies first?

At the end of life, organs shut down at different rates. For instance, the lungs typically cease working before the heart stops completely. In some people, the brainstem stops functioning before other organs. This is known as brain death. However, research suggests some brain function may continue for up to 10 minutes after death.

### How long does a person's body stay warm after death?

The body begins to get colder immediately, but body temperature drops slowly, at a rate of 1.5 degrees F per hour.

### What do they do with a person's body when they die?

Normally, the body is transported to a morgue or mortuary. Depending on the circumstances of the death, an autopsy may be performed. The body is then usually taken to a funeral home.

The funeral home prepares it to be viewed by friends and family or makes it ready for burial or cremation. The body is washed and disinfected. It's usually embalmed and stored at a cool temperature.

The above information is reprinted with kind permission from Verywell Health.
© 2022 Dotdash Media, Inc

www.verywellhealth.com

# Death: how long are we conscious for and does life really flash before our eyes?

An article from *The Conversation*.

THE C⬤NVERSATION

By Guillaume Thierry, Professor of Cognitive Neuroscience, Bangor University

The first time I reached past the sheer horror of the concept of death and wondered what the experience of dying may be like, I was about 15. I had just discovered gruesome aspects of the French revolution and how heads were neatly cut off the body by a Guillotine.

Words I remember to this day were the last of Georges Danton on April 5, 1794, who allegedly said to his executioner: 'Show my head to the people, it is worth seeing.' Years later, having become a cognitive neuroscientist, I started wondering to what extent a brain suddenly separated from the body could still perceive its environment and perhaps think.

Danton wanted his head to be shown, but could he see or hear the people? Was he conscious, even for a brief moment? How did his brain shut down?

On June 14, 2021, I was violently reminded of these questions. I set off to Marseille, France, having been summoned to Avignon by my mother because my brother was in a critical state, a few days after being suddenly diagnosed with terminal lung cancer. But when I landed, I was told my brother had passed away four hours ago. An hour later, I found him perfectly still and beautiful, his head slightly turned to the side as if he was in a deep state of sleep. Only he was not breathing anymore and he was cold to the touch.

No matter how much I refused to believe it on that day, and during the several months that followed, my brother's extraordinarily bright and creative mind had gone, vaporised, only to remain palpable in the artworks he left behind. Yet, in the last moment I was given to spend with his lifeless body in a hospital room, I felt the urge to speak to him.

And I did, despite 25 years of studying the human brain and knowing perfectly well that about six minutes after the heart stops, and the blood supply to the brain is interrupted, the brain essentially dies. Then, deterioration reaches a point of no return and core consciousness – our ability to feel that we are here and now, and to recognise that thoughts we have our own – is lost. Could there be anything of my beloved brother's mind left to hear my voice and generate thoughts, five hours after he had passed away?

## Some scientific experiments

Experiments have been conducted in an attempt to better understand reports from people who have had a near death experience. Such an event has been associated with out-of-body experiences, a sense of profound bliss, a calling, a seeing of a light shining above, but also profound bursts of anxiety or complete emptiness and silence. One

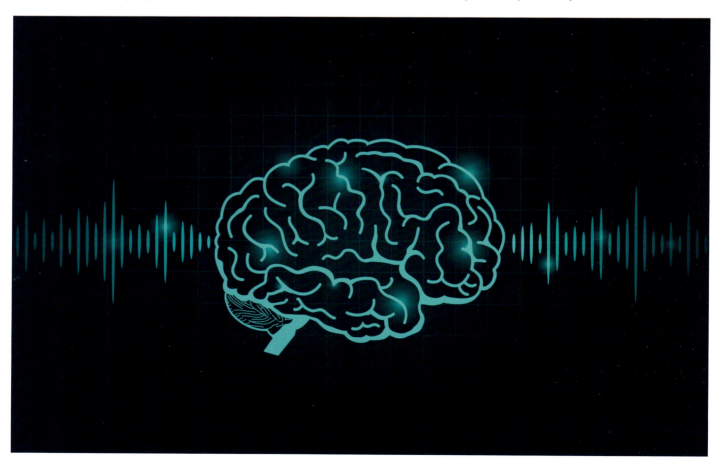

key limitation of studies looking into such experiences is that they focus too much of the nature of the experiences themselves and often overlook the context preceding them.

Some people, having undergone anaesthesia while in good shape or having been involved in a sudden accident leading to instant loss of consciousness, have little ground to experience deep anxiety as their brain commences to shut down. On the contrary, someone who has a protracted history of a serious illness might be more likely to get a rough ride.

It isn't easy to get permissions to study what actually goes on in the brain during our last moments of life. But a recent paper examined electrical brain activity in an 87-year-old man who had suffered a head injury in a fall, as he passed away following a series of epileptic seizures and cardiac arrest. While this was the first publication of such data collected during the transition from life to death, the paper is highly speculative when it comes to possible 'experiences of the mind' that accompany the transition to death.

The researchers discovered that some brain waves, called alpha and gamma, changed pattern even after blood had stopped flowing to the brain. 'Given that cross-coupling between alpha and gamma activity is involved in cognitive processes and memory recall in healthy subjects, it is intriguing to speculate that such activity could support a last "recall of life" that may take place in the near-death state,' they write.

However, such coupling is not uncommon in the healthy brain – and does not necessarily mean that life is flashing before our eyes. What's more, the study did not answer my basic question: how long does it take after the cessation of oxygen supply to the brain for the essential neural activity to disappear? The study only reported on brain activity recorded over a period of about 15 minutes, including a few minutes after death.

In rats, experiments have established that after a few seconds, consciousness is lost. And after 40 seconds, the great majority of neural activity has disappeared. Some studies have also shown that this brain shutdown is accompanied by a release of serotonin, a chemical associated with arousal and feelings of happiness.

But what about us? If humans can be resuscitated after six, seven, eight or even ten minutes in extreme cases, it could theoretically be hours before their brain shuts down completely.

I have come across a number of theories trying to explain why life would be flashing before someone's eyes as the brain prepares to die. Maybe it is a completely artificial effect associated with the sudden surge of neural activity as the brain begins to shut down. Maybe it is a last resort, defence mechanism of the body trying to overcome imminent death. Or maybe it is a deeply rooted, genetically programmed reflex, keeping our mind 'busy' as clearly the most distressing event of our entire life unfolds.

My hypothesis is somewhat different. Maybe our most essential existential drive is to understand the meaning of our own existence. If so, then, seeing one's life flashing before one's eyes might be our ultimate attempt – however desperate – to find an answer, necessarily fast-tracked because we are running out of time.

And whether or not we succeed or get the illusion that we did, this must result in absolute mental bliss. I hope that future research in the field, with longer measurements of neural activity after death, perhaps even brain imaging, will provide support for this idea – whether it lasts minutes or hours, for the sake of my brother, and that of all of us.

*4 March 2022*

# The perception and impact of death

An extract from *The YouGov Death Study*.

## How often do people think about death?

The YouGov Death Study shows that 9% of Britons report thinking about death – either their own or in general – at least once a day, and another 20% think about it several times during the week. On the opposite end are 7% who say they think about this less than once a year, and 4% say they never think about death.

It is of course worth noting that thoughts of death might be more common now – in the middle of a pandemic – than they would be in more normal times.

Currently, Britons aged 16-24 are twice as likely (12%) than those 60 or older (6%) to report thinking about death on a daily basis, with 25-59 year olds sitting in between at 10%.

When it comes to those religious Britons who are actively practising their faith, 13% report thinking about death once a day, compared to 8% of those who are not practising their religion or are not religious at all.

## When is the right time to teach children about death?

As death is likely to continue to be a part of human life for the time being, we asked Britons when the right time is to start introducing children to the concept of death.

Results shows that 13% of Britons think this should be done by the age of three, three in ten (29%) think this should be between the age of four and seven, while 7% think this should be between the ages of eight and nine. One in seven (15%) think children should first be taught about death when they are 10 or older.

## There are worse things than death, say Brits

Two-thirds (65%) of Britons think there are things that are worse than dying. There is a notable difference between younger and older Britons when it comes to this issue: while 72% of 16-24-year-olds say there are things which are worse than death, this falls to 59% among those 60 and older.

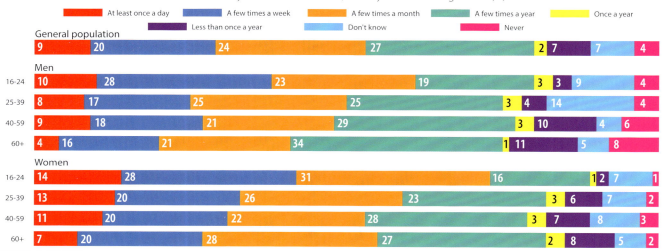

**How often do Britons think about death?**
How often do you think about death, either your own or in general? (%)

Source: YouGov - 19 - 23 March 2021

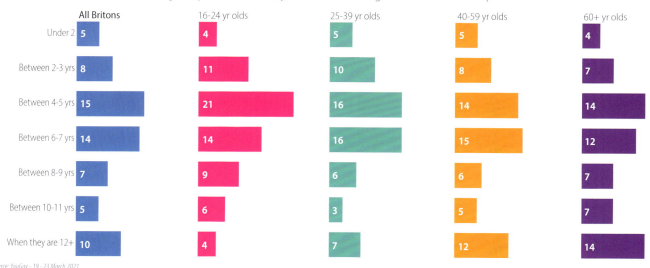

**When should you start teaching children about death?**
At what age do you think should you start introducing children to the concept of death? %

Source: YouGov - 19 - 23 March 2021

## Is there a fate worse than death?

Is there anything worse than death? (%)

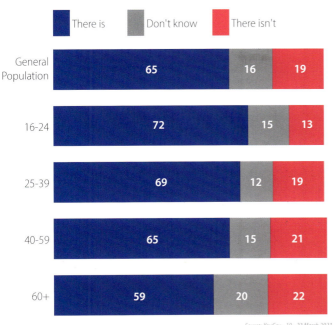

■ There is  ■ Don't know  ■ There isn't

| | There is | Don't know | There isn't |
|---|---|---|---|
| General Population | 65 | 16 | 19 |
| 16-24 | 72 | 15 | 13 |
| 25-39 | 69 | 12 | 19 |
| 40-59 | 65 | 15 | 21 |
| 60+ | 59 | 20 | 22 |

Source: YouGov - 19 - 23 March 2021

## Two in five people say the death of someone has made them appreciate life more

How, if at all, has the death of someone impacted your life? (%)

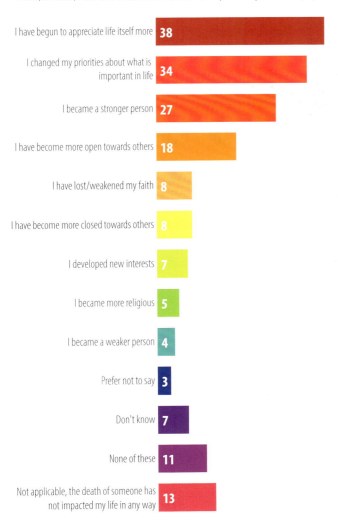

| | |
|---|---|
| I have begun to appreciate life itself more | 38 |
| I changed my priorities about what is important in life | 34 |
| I became a stronger person | 27 |
| I have become more open towards others | 18 |
| I have lost/weakened my faith | 8 |
| I have become more closed towards others | 8 |
| I developed new interests | 7 |
| I became more religious | 5 |
| I became a weaker person | 4 |
| Prefer not to say | 3 |
| Don't know | 7 |
| None of these | 11 |
| Not applicable, the death of someone has not impacted my life in any way | 13 |

Source: YouGov - 19 - 23 March 2021

Among Britons who are not comfortable talking about death, three in ten (31%) say there isn't anything worse than passing away. This is twice as many as those who say they are comfortable talking about mortality (17%).

### What impact has the death of another had on Brits?

When asked how the death of someone has impacted them, the most common response, at 38%, was that Britons began to appreciate life more itself, with this view being shared more by women (40%) than men (35%).

A third (34%) say they changed their views on what is important in life, while for 27% somebody's passing made them feel stronger. Just under one in five (18%) said they became more open to others after experiencing someone's death. One in eight (13%), however, say that the death of someone had no impact on them in any way.

Notably more women (31%) than men (21%) say that somebody's death made them stronger. Women are also more likely than men to report that they changed their priorities in life (38% vs 30%) having experienced someone dying. Conversely, more men (16%) than women (10%) say that they've not been impacted in any way following somebody's death.

While just 5% of the population say they have become more religious after experiencing somebody's death (with 8% saying their faith has weakened), 20% of practising religious Britons said their faith was strengthened following a death.

*6 October 2021*

# Talking about death

Why is it so hard to talk about death? We are all going to die one day, some of us sooner than others. However, there is still a huge taboo about talking about death, especially in Western countries.

However, it is important to have these conversations. By the time you – or your friend, partner or relative – are terminally ill, it may be too late or too hard to think about what you or they really want. When someone is in a coma in intensive care is not the time to be wishing that you had spoken to them about when they wished treatment to stop, or where they wanted to die.

This is a taboo that we urgently need to break down, as a society. This page discusses how you might start to have those conversations.

## In this world, nothing can be said to be certain but death and taxes. – Benjamin Franklin

### Why talk about death and dying?

There are a number of important reasons why you should have conversations about death and dying. They include:

**1. Most of us have an idea about how we would like to go, and family and friends would like to respect this**

For example, many people have thought about whether they wish to receive all possible medical treatment, and at what point they want treatment to stop. They have also often considered if they want to die at home, in a hospice or in hospital. If you don't talk about it, you won't know how your parents, relatives or partner wanted to be treated.

**2. There may not be time to have the conversation 'then'**

We all want to think that we're immortal – or at least that we are going to live a long time. The reality is, however, that we are all going to die, and it could be a lot sooner than you think. Life expectancy is much longer than it was in Victorian times, but you could have a car accident, be run over, or

be diagnosed with a terminal illness tomorrow. If you are unconscious, your relatives will not know your wishes unless you have discussed them beforehand.

**3. It is not good to be making difficult decisions under pressure**

When someone is seriously ill or injured, especially if it happens suddenly, everyone around them is upset and stressed. That is not a good recipe for calm, rational decision-making. If you have discussed your wishes beforehand, and talked about them with your loved ones–or even made decisions together about what you would like to happen– it is much easier for all of you, and for the medical staff providing treatment.

A simple example of this is organ donation.

## Organ donation: the importance of talking

Do you know what the legal position is on organ donation in your country?

Are you in an 'opt-in' system, or do you have a presumption of consent to donate without opt out?

Do you know if your relatives have opted in or out?

You will only have a few hours at most to make a decision about organ donation–and you do not want to find yourself taken by surprise at that time.

Talk early and often about these choices. Make sure you know what your relatives want–and that they know about your wishes too.

### What should you discuss?

Talking about death is hard. It may be easier to keep things practical and focused on particular issues, rather than try to have a general conversation. So, what exactly do you need to discuss?

It is important that you think and talk about two broad aspects: end-of-life care and treatment, and after death.

### End-of-Life Care and treatment

Ideally, many of us would probably say that we would like to die peacefully in our sleep, in our own homes. Unfortunately, very few of us are given this option.

The reality is that an awful lot of people die in hospitals or hospices every year, simply because their families are unable to provide the nursing care that they need. It may be helpful to consider where you want to die, and how important this is to you, because this will affect your family's decision-making.

You may also find it helpful to discuss questions about how long you want doctors to prolong treatment, especially if you are unconscious. If you have particular religious beliefs that mean that you do not want certain treatments, it is wise to make those clear.

## A doctor's perspective

In an article published on the Royal College of Anaesthetists' website in March 2020, consultant anaesthetist Dr. Helgi Johannsson explained why everyone should talk about death.

'There comes a point where we are certain that our efforts will not save our patient's life, and to continue treatment is simply adding to their pain and distress...

'It is nobody's wish to die on an intensive care unit... Most people will have shied away from having that conversation with their loved ones because they don't want to be morbid, upset themselves, frighten their loved ones, or there's never really been the right time. I want to ask you please, make now the right time... It is the greatest gesture of love you can give them [your family] and will make their discussions with us so much gentler and easier.'

## Case study: A letter from the past

Some five years before their aunt died, Sally and her brother John had both received a letter from her. In it, she said that she had written her will, and left the house to them both as she had no children of her own. The letter said:

'You know that I have resisted any suggestion that I should develop the bottom of the garden. However, when I'm gone, I won't care. I think that the property will probably be more valuable if you sell it to a developer, and what I want is for you two to get the most money from it.'

After their aunt's death, Sally and John instructed a local estate agent to put her house on the market. They also asked him about the possibility of selling to a developer. He looked a bit doubtful, then said,

'I had some contact with your aunt over the years. She specifically told me that she didn't want to sell the garden to a developer. I don't know if you knew about her wishes.'

Sally smiled at him. 'Thank you,' she said. 'She actually wrote to both of us a few years ago. She said that she wouldn't sell to a developer herself, but when she'd gone, we were to get the best price for the house, whether that was from a developer or not.'

The agent smiled back.

'That sounds like your aunt, all right! OK, I will put out some feelers to developers and market it direct too. We'll see where we get to.'

Problem solved–and all by a simple letter from the past.

---

You may also wish to consider who you would like informed that you are ill and/or dying.

Similarly, if you have relatives or friends in hospital, it may be helpful to ask if there is anyone they would like to see and/or speak to.

### After death

It may seem odd to be worrying about your wishes after you have died, but many people feel very strongly about their funeral arrangements and the disposal of their estate.

The first and most important issue is to make a will that clearly sets out your wishes.

The second is to tell your family and the beneficiaries what is included in your will.

Ideally, tell them all the detail, including why you have made that decision. Tell them who you have appointed as executors–and make sure that you have asked the executors if they are prepared to act.

### A professional executor?

Many, if not most, lawyers are prepared to act as executors of wills. If you appoint your solicitor as executor, he or she will almost certainly do a good job of delivering your wishes.

However, the fees for this service will be taken out of your estate, and the beneficiaries will end up with less money.

You may therefore prefer to appoint a friend or family member to carry out the job. Some people also ask a local religious leader to take on the task, especially if they have very few family members left.

It is also helpful to include any particular requests for your funeral arrangements in your will–and tell your family.

If you really don't care what happens at your funeral, it can be helpful to say that too. This will avoid endless arguments in the family about 'What Mum/Dad/Uncle Joe/Auntie Edna would have wanted'– because they all know that you wanted them to do as they wished.

If you don't feel able to have a full family discussion–or even any discussion at all–about your will and your wishes, it may be helpful to send a letter to everyone explaining why you have made your decisions. You may also wish to say that you don't want to discuss them any further.

This can also be useful for dealing with problems later, because everyone will know your thinking. If any questions arise, they can draw on that knowledge.

### Present discomfort can help in the future

It may feel uncomfortable talking about death. Few of us want to admit that we, or anyone we love, might actually be mortal. However, a little discomfort in the present can mean a much easier experience in future, and being able to meet someone's wishes about their death.

**It seems well worth overcoming the taboo, and simply having the necessary conversations.**

# Do I really need a will?

Having a legal document in place means you can state exactly what happens when you die – don't leave it too late.

By Rebecca Goodman

**W**e've heard it all before. We risk nightmare scenarios after our death if we don't have a will, from the wrong people getting their hands on our hard-earned cash to our children being left nothing. At least that's what experts warn us.

But am I really jeopardising my family's future because I don't have one? Or are these scare tactics just another way of getting us to pay for services we may not need, especially if we don't own a home?

Having a legal will means you can state exactly what happens when you die, from where your house will go, what will happen at your funeral, and who will become your children or pets' legal guardians.

But 49 per cent of us don't have one, according to research from charity will-writing scheme Will Aid, and it's pretty low down the list of life admin for most of us.

In fact, until very recently it had been one of those things I had been avoiding. I don't own a house yet and therefore had always dismissed it as a thing to do when I get onto the property ladder.

I'm married so my husband would inherit everything I own and he would be the one looking after our child, and two cats.

So, what would be the point in writing a will? Actually a whole range of reasons I'd not given much thought to.

If he also died at the same time, what happens next? Would our assets go straight to our daughter and who would arrange this? More importantly, who would become her guardian and would our cats be turfed out onto the streets?

A third of parents haven't named a legal guardian for their children, according to Will Aid.

If you don't have a will, you have no say over these things and while it's easy to assume the person you had in mind to inherit your assets and look after your dependents would do it, there are no guarantees this will happen.

When it comes to children, for example, a court will actually decide legal guardians if there is no will in place.

It also saves those left behind a whole admin headache. When someone dies it's not only extremely upsetting and emotional, there's also usually a lot of paperwork to wade through. Having a will is one way to save your family from any extra stress at this time.

When you write a will you not only state who will inherit your assets, you can also add details about where your money is, if there's someone in particular you'd like to pass along something specific to, and your wishes for your funeral.

A will can also be a tool when it comes to inheritance tax as no tax will be due on money and assets left to a spouse.

It becomes an especially important document if you're not married or in a civil partnership. For those living together without one of these official documents, partners have no legal right to any assets. In the worst-case scenario this could mean having to move out of a home you own together and losing joint savings at an already distressing time.

You can either go to a solicitor or use an online will-writing service. The cost is generally cheaper for online companies but they are largely unregulated. With a solicitor, for example, they will be regulated by the Solicitors Regulation Authority (SRA). You can complain directly if you have an issue or escalate the problem to the Legal Ombudsman.

Most online will-writing services do not have this layer of protection so if you do go for one of these, pick one which is a member of an official organisation such as the Society of Will Writers (SWW) or the Society of Trust and Estate Practitioners.

For a straightforward will, an online company should be able to provide everything you need at a reasonable cost, but if you have a more complicated situation such as children from different partners, or assets in other countries, it could be worth seeking out a solicitor.

Wills also need to be updated when life events happen, such as marriages, divorces, or if your financial situation changes.

November marks Will Aid's charity drive, which supports the work of nine UK organisations. Throughout the month participating solicitors write basic wills for people in exchange for a voluntary donation to the campaign, which will then be sent on to the charities.

It's a chance to get a will written at a discounted price as the campaign asks for a donation of £100 for a single will and £180 for mirror wills for a couple.

Lorraine Robinson, head of legal for Farewill, said: 'Even if you don't own property and you think you have nothing worth inheriting, if you don't have a will the laws of intestacy will determine how any belongings you have will be distributed and it could be left up to the courts to decide who will be responsible for caring for your children.

'Unmarried couples don't inherit anything when their partner dies in the UK, so it's really important to have a will in place to set out your wishes. It's also a way of passing on sentimental items or messages to those closest to you, and remembering causes you care about as the intestacy rules don't leave anything to charities.

'Having a will that records what you want to happen when you die, and how you want to be celebrated at your funeral, can also help save your loved ones a lot of uncertainty and stress at a very difficult time.'

*3 November 2021*

# At what age should you make a will?

Kate Anderson of Wright Hassall advises people of all ages on the things they should be thinking about when considering whether to write a will.

## At what age can you write a will in the UK?

Although most people writing wills in the UK are older than 50, you can legally write a will from the age of 18 and there are many reasons to do so.

## What happens if you don't write a will?

A will controls how your 'estate' (your money, property and possessions) is dealt with and who benefits from it when you die. If you died without a valid will, then you would need to rely on the intestacy rules (written in law) and your wishes may not be carried out.

For example, if you were cohabiting and died without leaving a will, the intestacy rules would mean that the person you live with would not receive anything from your estate.

## Why should you write a will?

While most people prepare wills for the likes of tax planning and making it easier for loved ones to deal with an estate on death, there are other reasons why you should make a will which could apply to people from a range of ages:

**Children:** If you have children who are under 18 years old, you could use your will to appoint a legal guardian. If you and the other parent both die the guardian could take over responsibility for your children. Guardianship can also be used to protect the position of parents who don't have legal status, such as in surrogacy cases or same-sex parents.

The family court can also appoint guardians, and anyone can apply to become a guardian. Having a will in place, which appoints guardians, helps you to retain some control over the care of your children if you died.

**Funeral wishes:** In a will you can provide instructions concerning your funeral arrangements. For example, you might prefer to be cremated or buried, or wish to ensure that your religious practices are followed.

It is important to note that funeral wishes are not binding and therefore do not have to be followed by your executors (the person(s) dealing with your estate). They can, however, help avoid family disagreements or assist loved ones and reduce the stress involved in making these types of decisions.

**Pets:** You can nominate someone you trust to take care of your pet in your will. In addition, you could choose to leave money to the nominated person, so they would not be left out of pocket for the likes of food, grooming and veterinary expenses. This could be done by a trust or by a simple cash gift.

**Specific gifts:** Perhaps you have a family heirloom, such as wedding ring that you want your niece to inherit, or a collection of signed football shirts that you want your friend to receive. If you have any items that you want to go to specific people, a will can ensure this happens.

Instead of leaving a specific item, you may want to leave a set sum of money from your estate. A will also allows you to leave cash gifts like this and you could also choose to benefit charities in this way.

**Digital assets:** Digital assets could include photos, email accounts, social media accounts, cryptocurrencies, gaming accounts, music or film libraries and much more. They're not physical possessions but they may still hold sentimental or monetary value. You could appoint a specific person to deal with these assets or make other specific provisions for them.

**Protecting the inheritance:** If you have a dispute with someone or are separated from a partner and you do not want them to benefit from your estate, you could make a will to ensure this is clearly stated and name who should benefit instead. It is possible your will could be contested; however, it helps to set out your wishes and intentions if a claim was made.

**Property:** Another consideration is if and how you own your property. If you and a partner own your home as 'joint tenants' and you died, your partner would automatically own your home in their sole name. However, if you own the property jointly as 'tenants in common' your share of the property would form part of your estate and would pass to your beneficiaries in accordance with your will or the intestacy rules.

Rights can also be included in wills to allow for individuals to be able to live in a property for specified periods of time. This could provide security for them to be able to live in the property whilst also ensuring the asset ultimately passes to your chosen beneficiaries.

It is therefore important to check the ownership of your property and consider preparing a will to ensure that your wishes regarding your property on your death are fulfilled.

## When should you write a will?

In conclusion, rather than focusing on what age you should make a will, the best consideration is twofold: Firstly, you should review your overall wishes regarding your estate and secondly whether these wishes could be carried out effectively on your death, without a will.

*11 May 2020*

# What to do when someone dies

When someone important to you has died it can be very hard knowing what to do next.

## How to get a death certificate

After someone dies, one of the first things to do is get a Medical Certificate of Cause of Death to be able to register the death.

When a death is from known and natural causes, the doctor who was caring for the person will issue this certificate.

If the cause of death is unknown or is not natural, the doctor (or sometimes the police) will notify a coroner, and a post-mortem might be required. This means the Medical Certificate can't be issued straight away, and this can delay funeral arrangements.

The coroner's office will tell you what the cause of death was. If it is found to be from a natural cause you will be told how to make an appointment to register the death, otherwise there may be an inquest, except in Scotland where there are no inquests. There is more information about this on the Government's page on coroner services.

## How to register a death

Once you have the Medical Certificate of Cause of Death, you need to register the death in the area where the person died within five days, or eight days if you're in Scotland. To find out where to do this visit the Government page on finding a register office.

The registrar will ask you for details of the person that has died, as well as documents like their passport and utility bills. The registrar will then issue:

♦ Copies of the death certificate, as many as you need (note that there is a charge per certificate)

♦ A certificate of registration or notification of death (BD8) form for the Department of Work and Pensions

♦ A certificate for burial or cremation (also called a green form).

## Telling others about a death

The Tell Us Once service lets you inform several different government departments of the death at the same time. This helps to avoid over-payment of benefits and pensions, and reduces the number of phone calls you need to make. Note that it's not currently available in Northern Ireland.

You'll need to tell banks, utility companies, and landlords or housing associations yourself. If you are the husband, wife or civil partner of the person who has died and were living in a council property the tenancy will usually pass to you, giving you the right to stay in the property, but this is different for other family members.

You may be able to get benefits if your husband, wife or civil partner has died, or if you are bringing up a child whose parents have died.

If your right to live in the UK depends on your relationship with the person who died, you might need to apply for a new visa. Check whether this applies to you on the Government website.

## What else you need to do

Once you have the death certificate, you can arrange the funeral and manage the person's financial affairs, also known as their estate.

If you have been named the executor of the will you might have to deal with the money and property of the person who's died. You may need to apply for probate, which is a court order required to release the person's assets. To find out more about this visit the Citizens Advice guide to dealing with the financial affairs of someone who has died.

# How much does a funeral cost in the UK?

According to the annual *Cost of Dying Report* by SunLife, the average cost of a funeral in the UK has increased by 1.7% to £4,184, with the average 'cost of dying' now at £9,263.

## How much does a funeral cost?

SunLife's annual Cost of Dying Report for 2021 shows that the average cost of a UK funeral is £4,184, a 1.7 per cent increase from the previous year and up 128% since 2004.

SunLife has been tracking funeral costs in their annual 'Cost of Dying' reports since 2007. For their 2021 report, they made some changes to how the average cost of a funeral is calculated. It's now weighted by the percentage of burials and cremations in the UK. To give a consistent comparison of funeral costs over time, previous year's figures were updated using the same methodology.

To calculate the £4,184 figure, SunLife define basic funeral costs as including:

◆   cremation or burial fees

◆   doctor fees

◆   funeral director fees

◆   minister or celebrant fees

## What is the cost of dying in the UK?

The 2021 report shows that the total cost of dying in the UK is £9,263, an all-time high. The cost of dying includes:

◆   the funeral

◆   professional fees

◆   optional extras like the wake or gathering

The 2020 cost of dying was up 0.8 per cent since 2019 and has risen 39 per cent in the last decade. The main reason for this is a rise in funeral costs. According to SunLife, the £4,184 average cost of a funeral makes up 45.2 per cent of the total cost of dying.

## What is the most popular type of funeral in the UK?

According to the report, of funerals in 2020:

◆   59% were cremations

◆   26% were burials

◆   14% were direct cremations (an unattended cremation without a funeral service)

Burials are still the most expensive funerals in the UK, now costing £5,033 on average and up by 1.2 per cent in the last year, while average cremation costs were also up by 0.7 per cent at £3,885. However, direct cremations now cost £1,554 on average, down 4.4 per cent since 2019.

Once again, London is still the most expensive place to die with funerals costing £5,235 on average. However, the biggest rise in cost was seen in the South East & East of England with costs up 9.8 per cent from 2019. Northern Ireland is again the cheapest place to have a funeral in the UK, with average costs 23 per cent below the national average.

## How did COVID-19 affect funerals in 2020?

Unsurprisingly, the COVID-19 pandemic affected funerals in 2020, with the number of direct cremations increasing by 11 per cent during February to July.

Of the people surveyed:

◆   82 per cent said the funeral they organised was affected by COVID-19

◆   71 per cent noted that not everyone who wanted to attend a funeral could due to social distancing guidelines

◆   86 per cent said there were things they couldn't do or had to cut back on

*14 January 2021*

# How to deal with the cost of dying

Against the unrelenting backdrop of Covid-19, here's how to navigate the financial side of bereavement.

By Rebecca Goodman

As the first unwelcome anniversary of Covid clicks round, official figures show more than half a million people have passed away in the UK since last March, including over 100,000 excess deaths.

And while the last thing we need to deal with at such a time is paperwork and bills, new figures reveal funeral costs hit a record high of £9,263 last year, while separate data point to long delays and administration errors heightened by the pandemic.

The average cost of a basic funeral which includes cremation or burial, and the fees for a doctor, funeral director, and a minister or celebrant, was £4,184 last year. That's a rise of almost 130 per cent in the last decade, according to new data from SunLife.

The cost ranges from £3,885 for a cremation to £5,033 for burial. But the total cost of the funeral, including extras such as flowers, food, a wake or gathering, and transport was £9,263.

More than a third of families have no savings for such high bills, the survey found, and more than one in 10 of those already dealing with the emotional impact of bereavement said the cost of a send off caused them notable financial problems. A quarter of those faced with this kind of bill used a credit card to pay with 25 per cent borrowing the money from someone else.

## So what are the options for funeral funds?

You could put money into a savings account specifically to go towards these costs, informing friends and family so they know what you would like to happen when you die.

There's also the option of a pre-paid funeral plan. These allow you to pay in advance for the funeral, either in a lump sum or regular payments over a set period, which isn't counted as part of your estate for inheritance tax purposes when you die.

Not all costs will be covered under these plans and, crucially, most of these plans are not protected by the Financial Services Compensation Scheme (FSCS). If the company were to go bust at any point in the hopefully long period before the money is needed, the funds could be lost.

If the death is sudden, funeral costs can also be covered by the deceased person's estate or through a life insurance plan. When someone dies, money specifically for the funeral can usually be released from their estate when the death has been registered.

Those on low incomes may also be able to get help paying with the costs with a funeral expenses payment of up to £1,000 from the government, although this usually has to be paid back at a later date.

Meanwhile, making a will can make the entire process slightly more straightforward for those left behind. Despite a surge in will writing thanks to the pandemic, around 40 per cent of people do not have one.

In your will you can state what you would like to happen when you die, who you want to look after your finances, and who the executor of your estate will be. If there is no will the deceased person's closest living relative is usually made the executor, which may not be their partner if they're not married or in a civil partnership.

The executor will also need to tell a long list of companies about the death, from financial institutions to household utility firms. There are a few systems set up to make this easier, including Tell us Once, the government's scheme whereby you only have to notify it once about the death and it then informs all other government organisations about the death.

A free service, Settld, works in a similar way but for private companies. Launched last week, it was prompted by the personal experiences of Vicky Wilson, co-founder and chief executive officer.

'After losing my grandmother 18 months ago, my mother and I were left closing all of her accounts,' she says.

'It was a terrible process of saying "My grandma has died" multiple times to multiple companies and then having to chase them up. While some businesses get it right, too many get it wrong and add unnecessary stress to those who need it least.'

However, despite the measures put in place to help the bereaved, mistakes often happen and financial institutions have repeatedly faced criticism over how they deal with those in mourning.

New research from consumer group Which? shows that bereaved families are facing severe delays and costly administration errors when settling their loved ones' finances after death.

It asked 1,600 people their experience of acting as an executor. Many said they had faced delays, admin errors, and poor knowledge when dealing with banks, and these had increased since the start of the coronavirus pandemic.

The survey found 17 per cent of people waited more than three months before they could close a loved one's bank account, rising to 37 per cent for those who began probate last year.

Almost a fifth of the bereaved report that it has been very difficult to contact a financial provider during and after lockdown, compared with just 3 per cent before March 2020.

Many mistakes made by the banks have left people out of pocket too, including one woman who had to pay £4,000 in funeral fees herself because her father's bank had lost his death certificate, the group warned.

'Unacceptable mistakes by banks [are] cropping up again and again during the probate process, leaving bereaved customers even more distressed and potentially out of pocket because of avoidable errors and delays,' says Jenny Ross, Which? Money editor.

'Banks must ensure they treat executors with compassion by communicating sensitively and making sure their processes are as efficient as possible.'

*17 February 2021*

# What is bereavement?

**B**ereavement is the experience of losing someone important to us. It is characterised by grief, which is the process and the range of emotions we go through as we gradually adjust to the loss.

Losing someone important to us can be emotionally devastating - whether that be a partner, family member, friend or pet. It is natural to go through a range of physical and emotional processes as we gradually come to terms with the loss. See our page (on the mind.org.uk website) on experiences of grief for information about the types of feelings that are common during the grieving process.

Bereavement affects everyone in different ways, and it's possible to experience any range of emotions. There is no right or wrong way to feel. Feelings of grief can also happen because of other types of loss or changes in circumstances, for example:

♦ the end of a relationship

♦ the loss of a job

♦ moving away to a new location

♦ a decline in the physical or mental health of someone we care about.

## Are there different types of grief?

In addition to the feelings of grief that you will experience following a loss, there are also other types of grief that you may experience at different times during bereavement.

## Anticipatory grief

Anticipatory grief is a sense of loss that we feel when we are expecting a death. It features many of the same symptoms as those experienced after a death has occurred, including depression, extreme sadness or concern for the dying person. It does not necessarily replace, reduce or make grief after the loss any easier or shorter, but for some people it can provide the opportunity to prepare for the loss and for what the future might look like.

## Secondary loss

After any loss you may also feel what is known as 'secondary loss'. After the initial shock of losing a loved one you may struggle when thinking of future experiences that those people will not be there to share or see, such as watching your children grow up, meeting partners or attending key life events like weddings.

> **'Bereavement is tough. All the "happy times" that have followed Ruth's death are tinged with a deep sadness for me.'**

## How long does grief tend to last?

There is no time limit on grief and this varies hugely person to person. The time spent in a period of bereavement will be different for everybody and depends on factors such as the type of relationship, the strength of attachment or intimacy to the person who died, the situation surrounding their death, and the amount of time spent anticipating the death.

*July 2019*

# How long does grief last?

There is no timeline for how long grief lasts, or how you should feel after a particular time. After 12 months it may still feel as if everything happened yesterday, or it may feel like it all happened a lifetime ago. These are some of the feelings you might have when you are coping with grief longer-term.

### *Learning to live with grief*

Learning to live with the loss of someone you love can take a long time, and just as everyone's grief is different, so each person feels differently as time passes after a bereavement.

### When will I feel better after a loss?

You and the people around you may have expectations about how quickly you should move on. But grief changes over time, as you understand how different your life is without the person. We are all different and there is no timetable or grief timeline for how long it will take you.

### The early stages of grief

In the early stages you may be caught up in a whirlwind of things that you need to do and sort out, or you may feel shocked and numb. After several months, the initial support you had from friends and family may start to fade. At the same time as people start to provide less support, you may find you start to feel less numb. Only as these things happen can you can start to experience how different your life is without the person you loved and start to grieve for that loss.

### The first year

It generally takes about a year to realise how much has changed in your life, both emotionally and practically. Some things only come up once a year, like celebrating a birthday or Christmas, or doing something the person who has died used to do, like renewing the car insurance. Each time one of these things happens, you are reminded of your loss, and your feelings of grief may come to the surface.

It may feel as if you are on an emotional roller coaster, where one minute you are coping and the next you feel overwhelmed by grief. You are likely to find you have some good days and some bad days.

As time passes, the balance between good days and bad days shifts and gradually you will find you have more good days and fewer bad days. But these changes are gradual, and each person is different, so the balance for you may not be the same as someone else after the same length of time.

Some of the physical symptoms of grief, such as having trouble sleeping and losing your appetite, also lessen over time. Taking care of yourself by eating well, getting some exercise and sleeping will help you to feel better in yourself and to cope.

### Two years on

Although the intensity of your feelings may lessen over time, there is no timetable for how long you will grieve. The length of time is different for each person. For most people their mourning period is a long process and it can

take years. After about two years you are likely to know the places, events and occasions that trigger your emotions. As you start to know these, you will also learn what helps you to cope with them.

After a while people around you – family, friends and colleagues at work – may forget what you have been through, or may encourage you to move on. You yourself may even feel that you ought to have moved on. But the goal is not to move on. Your grief is not something that can or should be 'fixed'. The goal is to find a way to live with and cope with your feelings.

You may eventually come to a point where your feelings of grief are a reminder of the person, and that in itself can be a source of comfort.

### Coping with grief longer-term

We have described below some of the feelings people have told us they experience over time. You may feel some or all of these and many other feelings too.

### I thought I was doing fine, but now I feel worse

There are lots of reasons why you might find that over time you feel your grief more rather than less. In the early stages, you may be caught up in a whirlwind of things that you need to do and sort out.

Friends, relatives and even work colleagues, are likely to be very conscious of what has happened and make time and effort to support you. But gradually things settle down and support from friends and relatives wanes. Only then do you have the time and space to understand how different your life is without the person you loved and to grieve for that loss.

You may find that you aren't able to grieve at first because you have caring responsibilities. For example, if you have young children or perhaps an elderly relative that you need to look after, your initial focus may be on supporting them.

Your own feelings of grief might be delayed after a bereavement. It may only be later that it feels real that the person has died, as you are able to make space for your own sense of grief. You may feel very angry at first. Feeling angry is very common, for example if your friend or relative was diagnosed late, but might have lived if they were diagnosed earlier, or if there were issues with their treatment.

At first you may focus on the aspects of the person's treatment or care that you were unhappy with. Your sense of anger may replace your grief. Those feelings of anger can stay for a long time. You may find that you don't want support or counselling at first but, as your feelings change over time, you may decide you do.

It is ok to ask for support when you need it, even if it is quite a long time after your friend or relative has died.

### Little things take me by surprise and suddenly I feel overwhelmed by grief

Over time, you will find a way to live with some of the more day-to-day reminders of the person you love. It is some of the unpredictable things, like a song on the radio, or finding one of their belongings in a drawer, that can trigger unexpected feelings. It can be particularly hard when this happens in public, for example, if you see someone's favourite cake in the supermarket.

Although it is completely normal to be upset, you might feel uncomfortable with being emotional in public. Unfortunately, it may make it harder that other people often don't know how to respond when this happens.

Although other people may not know how to handle it if this happens to you, and may pretend that they haven't noticed, it is not wrong for you to feel or act like this. In fact, it is completely understandable. Although it is hard, you shouldn't feel embarrassed.

### I want to talk about my partner, but others don't

One of the things you may find hardest to cope with is other people's reactions. Because people don't know what to say, they often avoid talking about the person who has died, or the feelings you might have. When you mention the person, they may seem awkward or ignore the comment. This can be extremely painful, as it can feel like they are behaving as if the person didn't exist. It can also feel very isolating, as you may feel embarrassed to mention the person, or 'out of sync' with the people around you.

However, your friend or relative was and will always be important in your life. You shouldn't feel bad that you might mention them in conversation or want to talk about them. Sometimes other people will take their lead from you. If you talk about your friend or relative, or explain that it is important to you that everyone still talks about them, it can help other people know how to respond. Support groups, such as our Online Bereavement Community, can really help as you can share your feelings – such as saying you still miss them – with people who empathise and don't judge.

> ### 'Rather than getting easier, my grief feels denser. I'm so tired - tired of trying to adjust to my situation, tired of feeling vulnerable, tired of feeling profoundly sad, tired of feeling fear, tired of feeling alone.'
>
> – 'Mentally, physically, emotionally exhausted' - a quote from our Online Bereavement Community

### People think I should move on, but I can't

It is common for other people, perhaps because they find it hard to cope with your grief, to encourage you to move on. People may even say that the person you loved would not have wanted you to still be grieving.

All these comments and some of the expectations and unintentional pressure applied by other people can make you feel as if you should have moved on in some way. But there is no timetable or timeline for grief. It is completely normal to feel profoundly sad for more than a year, and sometimes many years, after a person you love has died.

Don't put pressure on yourself to feel better or move on because other people think you should. Be compassionate with yourself and take the space and time you need to

grieve. You can't get over the death of someone you love and who has been important in your life in a year or to a set timeline. Your life has changed and can never be the same as it was when the person was alive.

How you feel depends on a range of things, including your relationship with them and your stage of life. It is completely normal to live with a deep sense of sadness. People sometimes make assumptions about what you should be doing or have done – like sorting out your friend or relative's belongings. They see these activities as markers of how 'well' you're doing.

But there is no right or wrong time for doing things. You should only do things at the time that feels right for you. You might choose to sort out your friend or relative's belongings a little at a time. You might do it after three months, six months, a year, three years or more. You may never do it, because having your friend or relative's belongings around you is a comfort to you.

Everyone is different and all of these are normal.

## Other people seem to be coping better than me

Comparing how you are feeling and coping with how you think other people are doing is a very common thing to do. You might compare yourself to another family member, or perhaps a neighbour whose husband has died. You might think that other people are coping or somehow doing better than you.

But it's important to remember that even though you may be mourning the same person, your relationship with them was different.

The practical aspects – like being their main carer or always phoning them on a Sunday – are different, and what you have lost is different. These differences mean you cannot compare your feelings to someone else's. You should also bear in mind that it is impossible to know how people are feeling or coping when they aren't with you. They may seem fine in public, but feel distressed in private. In other words, you need to be gentle with yourself.

Don't put expectations on yourself that you should be doing things in the same way or at the same time as other people seem to be.

## I can't face socialising or meeting up with friends

You may well find social activities such as meeting up with friends difficult. Sometimes, if it is your partner who has died, you may find it hard to go out with other couples, even though they may have been close friends. You may feel jealous that your friends are still a couple. Or it may be a painful reminder that your own partner is no longer there.

If it was a child – even a grown-up child, or grandchild – who has died, you may find it hard to hear others talking about their own children or grandchildren. You may worry that others won't want to be around you when you're miserable.

Or it may be that you just can't face going out. These feelings are all normal and most people experience them at some point. Eventually, if you never go out when people ask you, people may stop asking. In the short-term that may feel ok, but over time socialising with friends and not becoming too isolated can help you to cope. Rather than say 'no' every time, perhaps you can try to go out every other time someone asks you.

You can always let people know that you would like to see them, but may want to leave early. You may find it hard to be with a large group or to be around a lot of people, but feel you can cope better if it is only a couple of friends. You could let your friends know how you are feeling, and perhaps arrange to see only one or two people at a time. It may be hard to socialise because you don't have many friends or family around you.

For example, if your family live far away, or if you have been very focused on doing things as a couple, rather than with friends or a social group. When you already feel like you are struggling, building new friendships may feel like hard work. A group for people who are bereaved can be a good starting point for being able to share some of your feelings and ensuring that you do not become too isolated. A local group that shares some of your interests – whether that be handicrafts, walking or something completely different – can also be a good starting point.

## I feel overwhelmed by grief and just want it to stop

Sometimes your feelings of grief might be so painful that you feel overwhelmed. You may find it hard to see meaning or purpose in your life, and want to find a way to make it stop. It is not unusual to feel that you can't cope with the intensity of your grief, but most people can and do.

These very intense emotions are a normal response to the death of someone that you love and they can last a long time. If you feel you are not coping, or if you know the way you are coping is not good for you – for example if you are drinking alcohol heavily – you might want to get some help to cope.

That help might be talking with your GP or some form of prescription medicine, like antidepressants. Your GP is a good starting point, as they can refer you to support. If necessary they can prescribe medication that can take the edge off the intensity of your feelings, and that might help you if you are struggling to sleep.

## I can't talk to people about how I'm feeling

There are lots of reasons why you might find it hard to talk about how you're feeling. If you are not normally someone who talks about your emotions, you are not likely to start now.

But you may find that other people who are also grieving do want to talk about it, or want you to talk about it. When this happens you need to try to find a way to be sensitive to each other's needs, whilst coping with your feelings in your own way. When someone dies, relationships and communications within families can become strained. Sometimes families don't talk to each other about their emotions.

It may be that you would normally talk about things together, but you don't want to because you know you'll get upset or the person you're talking to will get upset. It can help if you

are able to find ways that you can talk. In other cases, it may be that you feel you can't talk about your feelings because other people won't understand, or because you feel they expect you to have moved on.

While no-one can understand exactly how you are feeling, you may find sharing your feelings and experiences with others at a support group or online can help.

## People don't think I should be grieving at all

Sometimes the nature of your relationship with the person who has died means that other people don't expect you to grieve. This often happens when your relationship was distant in some way. This might be because you hardly ever saw the person, had a difficult relationship with them or were estranged, such as if you were divorced from them.

If this is the case, your sense of grief may take you by surprise, and other people may also struggle to understand what you are feeling. Sometimes, perhaps because people didn't know you were in a relationship with the person, people may not realise you are grieving.

All these things may make you feel, and may make other people assume, that your grief is somehow not valid, or that your feelings should be less strong. When this happens you don't have the emotional support around you that other people normally get.

It may mean that you do not feel able to share your feelings with those around you, or openly grieve. It can be helpful to find another outlet for your feelings, such as bereavement counselling, a support group or an online community.

# Understanding the five stages of grief

You might have heard of the five stages. But what are they, and does grief really follow a set timeframe?

### Who developed the five stages of grief?

The five stages of grief model was developed by Elisabeth Kübler-Ross, and became famous after she published her book *On Death and Dying* in 1969. Kübler-Ross developed her model to describe people with terminal illness facing their own death. But it was soon adapted as a way of thinking about grief in general.

### Do the five stages happen in order?

The five stages – denial, anger, bargaining, depression and acceptance – are often talked about as if they happen in order, moving from one stage to the other. You might hear people say things like 'Oh I've moved on from denial and now I think I'm entering the angry stage'. But this isn't often the case.

In fact Kübler-Ross, in her writing, makes it clear that the stages are non-linear – people can experience these aspects of grief at different times and they do not happen in one particular order. You might not experience all of the stages, and you might find feelings are quite different with different bereavements.

## What are the five stages of grief?

### Denial

Feeling numb is common in the early days after a bereavement. Some people at first carry on as if nothing has happened. Even if we know with our heads that someone has died it can be hard to believe that someone important is not coming back. It's also very common to feel the presence of someone who has died, hear their voice or even see them.

### Anger

Anger is a completely natural emotion, and very natural after someone dies. Death can seem cruel and unfair, especially

when you feel someone has died before their time or you had plans for the future together. It's also common to feel angry towards the person who has died, or angry at ourselves for things we did or didn't do before their death.

### Bargaining

When we are in pain, it's sometimes hard to accept that there's nothing we can do to change things. Bargaining is when we start to make deals with ourselves, or perhaps with God if you're religious. We want to believe that if we act in particular ways we will feel better. It's also common to find ourselves going over and over things that happened in the past and asking a lot of 'what if' questions, wishing we could go back and change things in the hope things could have turned out differently.

### Depression

Sadness and longing are what we think of most often when we think about grief. This pain can be very intense and come in waves over many months or years. Life can feel like it no longer holds any meaning which can be very scary.

### Acceptance

Grief comes in waves and it can feel like nothing will ever be right again. But gradually most people find that the pain eases, and it is possible to accept what has happened. We may never 'get over' the death of someone precious, but we can learn to live again, while keeping the memories of those we have lost close to us.

### Are the five stages useful?

The five stages are useful for understanding some of the different reactions you might have to a death. But it's important to remember that every grief journey is unique.

It certainly doesn't mean that something is wrong if you experience a whole mess of different stages and emotions, or if you never pass through some of the 'stages.'

### Are the five stages still accurate?

Since the five stages were first developed, there have been lots of new ways of thinking about grief. At Cruse, our understanding has grown over the years, based on research into the best ways to help and understand bereaved people.

We now know there are many ways to experience grief and many models to help us understand bereavement. One we find can be helpful, is the idea of 'growing around your grief.' In this model, there are no set stages or phases to bereavement. Instead, your grief remains the same but, as you grow as a person, it starts to take up less space in your life.

# What are the 7 stages of grief?

By Julia Usher

**S**adly, every one of us will experience the pain of grief at some point in our lives. Losing a loved one or saying goodbye to a pet can be exquisitely painful, changing our world forever and throwing us into a tailspin.

You've probably heard of the different stages of grief, but you might not know how they work, or which one you're experiencing at any given time. Everyone grieves in their own way. However, knowing this and actually experiencing it are two very different things. It's very natural to feel alone in your grief or worry that you're not grieving 'normally.'

## Are there five or seven stages of grief?

The 'Seven Stages of Grief' model is based on the 'Five Stages of Grief', initially theorised in 1969 by Swiss psychologist Elizabeth Kübler-Ross. She attempted to classify the different emotions and thoughts that people experience after losing someone they love. Her original stages are listed with two more added in recent years to strengthen the model.

It's not always perfect, and you might go through some phases or emotions that aren't listed. After all, grief is non-linear and often messy. It's common to move up and down the ladder, progressing to the higher steps only to come crashing down, especially on anniversaries or other meaningful dates.

If this model doesn't work for you, or if you're not finding it useful or helpful, it's OK to kick it to the kerb and seek resources that work for you. But please don't try to avoid your grief. While pushing your despair to the back of your mind and ignoring it may seem like it's helping, this often prolongs the pain. Instead, allow yourself to grieve, heal, and work your way through the process.

It's not easy. In fact, it may be one of the most challenging experiences of your life. But it will get easier.

## What are the five stages of grief?

Although not everyone will experience the five stages of grief or may experience them in a different order, these stages of grief are:

♦ denial

♦ anger

♦ bargaining

♦ depression

♦ acceptance

## What are the 7 stages of grief?

Based on the five-stage approach, the seven stages of grief help explain the often complicated experience of loss. While you may not experience them all (or may experience them in a different order) these include:

♦ shock and disbelief

♦ denial

♦ guilt

♦ anger and bargaining

♦ depression, loneliness and reflection

♦ reconstruction (or 'working through')

♦ acceptance

We explain more about each of these stages, and what they may look like for you.

## The 7 stages of grief explained

### Shock and disbelief

When you first find out about the death of a loved one, your initial reaction might be shock or complete disbelief. You're not quite in denial, you just can't even parse what has just happened. This is a defence mechanism that is designed to protect from pain.

This stage can explain why we can plan a funeral or make other arrangements immediately after a death – you're in a state of suspension until you are able to grieve.

### Denial

While denial shares similarities to disbelief, it is its own coping mechanism and also helps you to deal with grief and pain. You might simply deny that your loved one is gone, or push the thoughts out of your head. Some people can get stuck in a pathological and chronic state of denial and refuse to admit that anything bad has happened, but this is rare.

This phase takes form in different ways. Some people will deny they are grieving or affected by the loss whilst others will deny their loved one has gone.

### Guilt

Guilt can feel like a punch to the gut. It's completely normal to wonder what you could have done to prevent the loss from happening. While most of us will feel some sort of guilt when a loved one dies (thoughts such as, 'I should have done more,' 'I should have called the doctor with my concerns' are common), around 7% of people will experience 'complicated grief.'

Complicated grief is often centred around guilt and causes the sufferer to ruminate endlessly about the details around the death and what they could have done differently. They also struggle to accept the finality of death, and/or surround themselves with photos and mementoes (such as a piece of memorial jewellery) that help them to believe the deceased is still with them.

### Anger and bargaining

This stage usually occurs after the ceremonies and funerals. The comforting family and friends have left you, and you're trying to go about your life as usual. That's often when the anger comes in, and often bargaining as well.

You might start to feel angry at the doctors, or another party, and perhaps even at the deceased themselves. This anger can often cause a person to feel even more guilt, but

know that it is entirely normal, and provides a necessary emotional release.

In some cases, people begin to 'bargain' mentally, even though they know it is in vain. For example, 'I would do X to have them back.'

## Depression, loneliness and reflection

Now that you have fully acknowledged the loss, it is common to experience depression and/or deep sadness. You may also feel lonely and isolated from other loved ones. This can be an especially poignant time to seek the help and guidance of a grief counsellor who can help you through the pain.

These sessions can be an opportunity for reflection about what your loved one meant to you, the true nature of your relationship, and how you can move on in the future.

## Reconstruction, or 'working through'

By this time, you may still find yourself moving up and down the ladder, but are building a new life without your deceased loved one and living a 'new normal.' The hurt may feel raw and painful, you now know that you cannot change the situation. Though you may not be fully ready to accept the death, you know that life has to go on.

## Acceptance

The final stage of this model is acceptance. You have worked through the most painful and difficult work of grieving, and you accept that your loved one is gone and that you need to continue living your life.

You may begin to find joy again and smile rather than wince or cry when you think of your loved one. You may join new clubs, start a new hobby, take a trip, or clear out their possessions, keeping only the most important mementoes.

## How long do the seven stages of grief last?

There is no set time for how long the process of grieving should last. For some people, the process may take several weeks. For others, it may be years. If you are worried that your grief may have turned into depression, there are signs you can look out for (see our website for more information).

## Grief is never easy

As time passes, you may find that you occasionally regress to one of the early stages, especially around holidays or anniversaries. However, over time it does become easier, and your pain will subside. It never goes away completely, but you can live with your loss.

Grieving in the time of the coronavirus has made things perhaps even more difficult than they usually are. With limitations and restrictions on hospital and care home visits, the rule of six and restricted numbers for funerals, our usual steps in saying goodbye to loved ones have changed.

It's not easy, but keep talking to those around you and share your feelings. Help is available and while it can feel incredibly lonely, you don't need to go through this alone.

*26 October 2020*

# A-Z of bereavement

## Anger

Anger is a very normal feeling when someone in your family has died. Angry at the person who has died, other people in the family, yourself, doctors, God.

## Bereaved

Being 'bereaved' is one way of describing what you are when someone close to you has died.

## Confusion

You might not understand grief – it is a confusing time for everyone. It can help to talk to someone else in your family, a teacher or a professional.

## Dreams

At a time when you really need to sleep, you may find yourself troubled by difficult dreams.

## Emotions

Your emotions will be all over the place when someone you care about has died. You may feel lots of different things – sad, angry, confused, worried, relieved, fed up. You may feel all of these at the same time.

## Funerals

Funerals give us a chance to say goodbye and are a time to think about the person who died. You may not be sure whether or not you want to attend. It's okay, either way.

## Guilt

Guilt is normal – it may follow if the bereaved person feels they could have acted differently and so prevented a death.

## Help

Lots of different people might say you should get some help. Help comes in lots of shapes and sizes and from many different people. You may not always think you need any help – and the time has to be right for you. But it can be helpful to talk to someone who really wants to listen to you.

## Information

Sometimes it helps to find out more information about things that are worrying you – if you know what you are dealing with then it can be easier to sort things out.

## Jokes

Don't feel bad. Laughter is normal and it's ok to laugh and tell jokes even after someone has died.

## Keepsakes

Sometimes it's nice to have keepsakes to remind you of the person who died. This might be something like a watch or ring, or maybe an item of clothing you always used to borrow and get into trouble for.

## Letting off steam

Sometimes your feelings can build up and explode, particularly angry feelings – so it's good to find a safe way of letting off steam.

## Missing

It's natural to miss someone after they have died. It is a big loss and often you will miss them when doing things you used to do together or something they liked to do.

## Not fair

It's normal to feel as though it's not fair when someone you care about has died. Why should it have happened in your

family? What did the person do wrong? What did you do wrong?

## Optimism

You may struggle to remain optimistic about the future when someone close has died. Your future is still important even though it may be very different to the life you had planned. Strive to hold on to your hopes and dreams for the future.

## Parents

Parents will be grieving too, especially if their partner or child has died. This means they are not always emotionally available to offer you the support you need.

## Questions

Everyone has questions when someone they care about has died. You might have questions about medical facts, about death, grief and your feelings. However, you may also have to accept that some questions, such as why someone chose to take their own life, can never be answered. It's difficult but not impossible to live with not knowing the answer.

## Relationships

Having had someone in your life die will change you as a person and some relationships may well be strained by this. It can sometimes be easy to lose touch with friends after someone has died.

## Suicidal feelings

After someone important has died, those left behind may sometimes have suicidal feelings – wondering what is the point of living without that person. It is important to talk through these feelings with someone you can trust to listen to how you are feeling; you can call the Samaritans at any time of any day (116 123).

## Talking

Talking helps. Talking about the person who has died, about what happened, about how you are thinking and feeling.

## Upset

Just about everyone who has ever been bereaved will feel upset. Feeling 'upset' has got within it bits of feeling sad, bits of feeling fearful, bits of feeling confused and bits of feeling as if everything has been taken and turned upside down.

## Vulnerable

Feeling vulnerable can come with being bereaved. You don't expect people close to you to die – especially if they were not old. The world can seem an unsafe, insecure place. It may make you worry more about other members of the family or about your own health.

## Why

Why – is a small word for the biggest question. Why they died? Why they died in the way they did? No one can really answer the 'why' questions; but it helps to have someone to listen while you ask them.

## X-tra

Being bereaved brings with it a lot of extra stuff. You may find yourself with extra responsibilities – more chores, looking after younger brothers or sisters. You may find yourself with extra worries or concerns. You may find yourself with extra stress. You may find yourself with extra-strong feelings, thoughts and reactions.

## Yelling

Yelling can help relieve some of your tension and frustration. It's normal and ok to lose your temper from time to time. You may find yourself yelling at those around you or you may find it helps to go off alone and yell at the sky. 'I kept on yelling at my family and friends, for no real reason.'

## Zzz… sleep

Zzz… sleep can be affected after a death in the family. You may find it's hard to get to sleep because when your head hits the pillow, you find yourself thinking about what has happened and how you feel.

# Why we can't stomach food when we lose a loved one

By Sabine Horner

The number of times I hear of bereaved people struggling with eating and asking others whether they have the same problem is staggering. But is it any wonder?

Not many people warn us of this effect of grief and, therefore, we are ill-prepared when we are suddenly confronted with a severe lack of appetite. Which may be okay initially. But when we have not been eating well for weeks and months, this eventually takes its toll on our health.

## So, what on earth is going on?

Not feeling hungry is one of our body's protective mechanisms when we are grieving. The powerful emotions that overwhelm us make it difficult for our body to process any food. Let alone the food many of us habitually eat - sandwiches, cereals with cold milk, wheat pasta, meat pies, macaroni cheese or pizza, to name just a few common dietary staples.

These foods are difficult to digest and we simply lack the energy and digestive strength to break them down.

## Here's why

Apart from being exhausting, grief triggers a massive stress response that diverts blood away from our digestive system into our limbs and the heart. Ever heard of the 'fight-and-flight' response? Well, grief is also perceived as a major threat. ●

Without sufficient blood in our stomach, food just sits there and starts to ferment, causing gas and bloating and other digestive issues.

But the problem can start higher up – in our mouth and throat.

## How many times do you simply forget to drink? Or put it off until later?

Saliva has an important digestive function and a dry mouth indicates that your whole digestive system is dry. This includes your stomach which needs to produce up to 2 litres of stomach acid every day. That's a lot when you are not drinking enough. Lack of fluids is another reason why food can feel like a heavy brick in your stomach. And why acid reflux is another common ailment after a major loss.

Our emotional stress response also causes tension all along the digestive tract. This affects the vagus nerve which is a two-way communication highway between our brain and our gut. And this can cause difficulty swallowing – among other problems.

I was fortunate that I happened to eat lots of dark chocolate after my husband died which contains substances that help relax the smooth muscles in the throat. But simply chewing a handful of fennel seeds also does the trick as I found out later.

## What else can help you eat better while your digestion is weak?

♦ To reduce stress and improve blood flow to your stomach, breathe deep into your belly before and after a meal. This stimulates the vagus nerve, putting you into rest-and-digest mode. This simple practice will also increase your digestive juices by up to 24%! Only eat cooked meals and drink warm fluids. Cold constricts blood flow as well.

♦ Keep meals small and easy to digest. 'Baby' food is best. Think of blended soups or stews, warm smoothies, stewed apples, or porridge.

♦ Add fresh ginger to everything you eat. And drink fresh ginger tea when you don't feel like having breakfast. Ginger improves appetite and helps relieve nausea, constipation, acid reflux and any other digestive issues.

♦ Drink a glass of warm water with a wedge of lime and a pinch of salt before a meal. Anything sour or salty makes our digestive system juicier and increases the flow of saliva.

*Author: Sabine Horner, Nutritionist and AtaLoss Ambassador, www.sabinehorner.com*

*AtaLoss provides the UK's bereavement signposting website www.ataloss.org*

# Digital legacies – are we ready to be surrounded by virtual ghosts?

By Emmie Harrison-West

In a tragic twist of fate, Lorna Harris lost both her parents, when they both died within months of each other.

Three years on though, she is still in 'contact' with her mum, Glenda, 71.

'I still have voice notes from her and I listen to them when I need to remember what she sounds like,' Lorna, 48, tells Metro.co.uk.

'I have one that I play a lot. It's so normal. I had flu and my parents were popping me some bits over to my house… My mum and dad are in their car and mum is saying she's got me "Lemsip, a magazine and a massive bar of chocolate. Will pop it over and give you a cuddle. Keep warm. Love you"…'

'I listen to it when I feel sad or ill,' adds Lorna. 'Not all the time but now and then. My dad Harry is in the background joking around that I am 'skiving off work' but they both shout 'love you' at the end.

'I love seeing videos and hearing their voices but sometimes the magnitude of their loss is pulled into full focus and can send me reeling a bit.'

While no longer considered a phenomenon of the modern world, voicemails can often hold a far deeper meaning than any of us realise – a chance to immortalise the unique sounds, breaths and intonations of a deceased loved one.

And they're not the only way someone can leave a digital legacy. Thanks to 21st-century technology, the dead are far from hidden these days. Family members can log onto their Facebook accounts to share updates about the deceased's lives, wishing they were there, as a form of contact; they archive and often print dead loved ones' WhatsApp messages, revisit Instagram Reels or listen to songs and videos they recorded in the past.

Nowadays we can easily carry the deceased around in our pockets, never quite deleting that mundane voicemail of a shopping list, or wiping their contact from our address books – constantly blurring the lines between what is real, and what we wished was still real.

Celebrities are in on the act too, with Kim Kardashian revealing on Instagram in 2020 that Kanye West gifted her a lifelike hologram of her late father, who died in 2003 from esophageal cancer.

Even our children are making contact with the dead – LBC radio presenter James O'Brien once shared on Twitter that his 10-year-old continued to message his deceased father, hoping that he had an amazing life, and informing him of birthdays and presents.

Talking about her own experiences of holding onto her parents' digital legacy, Lorna explains, 'Grief is very hard. We get through it how we can. I downloaded my mum's WhatsApps and printed them into a little folder. It's like a love letter from her – with moaning!'

'I have never called it digital ghosts,' she says, adding, 'but I suppose in some way it is.'

With research estimating that 8,000 Facebook users died daily in 2018, there's no doubt we are surrounded by online footprints of those who've passed. But while some use these digital legacies as a form of closure, and a chance to remind themselves of good times gone by, others question whether holding on to the past might be harmful to our grieving process – hindering us in our healing, rather than soothing our emotional wounds?

It's a question Sarah grapples with after being caught off guard via an unsolicited push notification from a gaming app.

After setting up Scrabble on her phone to keep a close friend company in hospital as he didn't want visitors, she hadn't anticipated the impact it would later have after he sadly passed away.

'My phone buzzed and my body froze,' she says, remembering the moment. 'I'd received a notification saying our online Scrabble game was over. When I saw his name, cold lightning went through me. I closed the app, deleted it and threw my phone at the floor.'

Recalling why she downloaded the app in the first place, Sarah explains, 'Playing online and sending texts and emails was all I could do. His turns in the game became fewer and far between.

'He hadn't responded to my last text when I heard he was in palliative care. I sent one final message, sending my love, telling him I missed him and was thinking of him. I couldn't bring myself to say goodbye.'

Now, Sarah says, her house 'is full of ghosts'.

'At my kitchen table where I made him cups of tea. In the armchair where he told me he was ill. The window where we hugged… I didn't know it would be the last time I would see him,' she says.

However, despite the initial shock of the app notification, Sarah admits she has found solace in other forms of their online communication.

'I didn't know who to contact when he'd gone, as I didn't really know his friends or family,' she says. 'Instead, I looked through our old texts and emails. I found comfort in every expression of hope and every smiling emoji he'd sent. His messages of affection warmed me when I felt numb.'

'My grief is confusing, noisy, and painful. It leaves me breathless. It's messy and I don't know where to keep it. Looking back over those digital whispers from the past offers a little solace. They keep small connections alive.'

But what happens if these digital connections are suddenly lost? Maybe through a change in phone providers, or a family member shutting down a Facebook page. Could it spark feelings of deep loss all over again?

According to some experts, the answer is yes – with psychologists calling this the fear and anxiety of 'second loss'.

While we know that photos and camcorder videos may fade and perish over time, social media (we believe) is expected to always be there – we're reliant on it being reliably present. So when that is removed, along with the black-and-white memories of our loved ones', we start to panic.

'For the bereaved, the Internet has become an important tool, which many find comforting,' Dr Debra Bassett, Visiting Fellow at the University of Bath and a digital afterlife researcher, explained in a 2018 paper. 'The Internet is providing a platform where "ordinary" people can remain socially active following biological death, which was once the realm of the rich and famous in society.

Speaking to Metro.co.uk, she adds, 'However, current research has highlighted that digital endurance is creating a new fear for the bereaved: Fear of losing the data created by – or commemorating – the deceased.'

Dr Bassett says she began research into the digital afterlife after her friend's daughter passed away, while leaving behind an active Facebook page. 'I grew interested in why people were still talking to her as though she was still alive,' she explains.

'My research has shown that people who "control" the digital memories and messages find comfort in them. Comfort and control are entwined – it has shown that virtual keepsakes are seen by the bereaved as containing what I call the "essence" of the dead in a way that physical keepsakes are not.'

That's why, Debra says, the fear of 'second loss' – a theory she originated – is one to be aware of. 'People are anxious about losing the precious data of the dead through technical obsolescence or lack of control – several participants told me how it would be like losing their loved ones all over again,' she says.

However, she warns that it's something we all should be prepared for losing, as Dr Bassett adds, 'Digital immortality does not exist – digital endurance only exists whilst the companies that hold the data exist.'

Sophia Waterfield, 32, admits that she'd be devastated if she lost the only recording she has of her late Grandma, after she died suddenly from a heart attack.

'It's a special video, apart from it being the only one I seem to have, as it features her trying to make my son laugh when he was around four or five months old,' explains Sophia, who listens to it several times a year, including the day her Grandma passed.

'I keep going back it because I want to hear her voice, remember how daft she was – and I mean that in the most loving way possible! – and also remember the times she bonded with my son when he was a baby. I have pictures of her, but the video is the only way I can hear her.'

Does she worry about losing that video? 'God, absolutely,' Sophia says emphatically. 'I don't think I would have anything else as close to her death as that. Old family videos perhaps, but nothing like that. I would probably be very sad every time I wanted to hear her.'

Thankfully, there are a growing number of organisations helping change the way we interact with the dead online, preserving their life like a 'virtual Victorian memory box,' according to founder of MyWishes, James Norris. Initially set up in 2013 as DeadSocial before changing its name, his site's aim was to preserve your social media and digital legacy – helping you 'tweet from beyond the grave'.

Jonathan Davies is a trustee for the memorial tribute charity MuchLoved, which also preserves digital legacies, as well as giving people the chance to fundraise for a chosen charity. With over a million registered users, the site has raised £100 million in donations for over 6,000 charities so far, he says.

Jonathan admits that his own experiences of grief had a profound impact on him.

'After my brother Philip died suddenly in 1995, I remember climbing over the fence of the graveyard one evening in order to visit his grave,' he remembers. 'It may have been a reaction to the idea of the cemetery gates closing shut at dusk, or simply the need I had at a particular time, regardless of whether it was day or night, to connect with him.'

Three years later Jonathan sadly lost his mum and recalls that it took many years before he was financially and emotionally able to begin work on a memorial website with his friend Andy Daniels.

When MuchLoved finally came to fruition in 2006, he says, 'It was really therapeutic for me designing and helping build the service. Looking back, it was something I needed, but did not exist when my brother died.'

Creating an online memorial service 'presents no geographical or time constraints,' adds Jonathan, and says that as well as recording key events and details of their life, the website can display personal memories that otherwise would be shut away from the light of day.

'Immediately following Phil's death, I wrote a poem that I read out at his funeral which I'm proud and happy to show on his tribute site today,' he recalls. 'My father also added his personal diary entries outlining his own grief experience.

'I have given close friends and family members the ability to access and contribute to my brother's memorial so that they can keep his memory alive in their own way, at the same time perhaps adding photographs or stories that I may not have seen or heard before.'

The chance to continually update a memorial over time is something that Jonathan says he finds particularly helpful. 'It never has to be completed or closed, as with my feelings for my dead brother,' he explains. 'It is this ongoing process of recording your thoughts and memories in many forms that can assist in your grieving, helping you connect with and keeping the memories of your loved one alive as you gradually adjust to life after loss.

'It does not matter whether these bonds, or digital shadows, are virtual or tangible, it just matters that they exist and they help.'

However, while he does believe that digital services can be 'an important tool' when it comes to grieving, Jonathan also points out that they 'should be seen as a complementary rather than an alternative way of grieving'.

'You can see how traumatic it has been for many families during the covid pandemic that they were not able to have the funeral ceremony or wake that they needed,' he explains.

'No digital service can replace that physical togetherness of an in-person gathering, however it can complement and assist – for example, enabling a funeral service to be streamed to someone that cannot attend, or providing a sensitive format for wider friends and colleagues to share memories and send their condolences.'

Whether it is good for us to keep loved ones alive in a virtual world, is a tricky question, according to Maria Bailey, founder of Grief Specialists, an online hub to connect grievers with professional support.

'I would say everyone grieves differently – if you want to listen to voicemails and read text messages, there's nothing wrong with that,' she says.

However, Maria does warn that if you have unanswered questions for a deceased loved one, it might become a problem to hold onto so-called digital ghosts if that person is no longer there to answer them.

'Some of our grief specialists run a short action programme called the Grief Recovery Method that is very effective in helping grievers deliver all the things left unsaid, which in turn helps to deal with the pain they're feeling,' she explains.

And, as Jonathan's story proves, not even the professionals who make alleviating grief their aim are exempt from the pain.

After discovering a voicemail from her mum, Gay Kennedy, following her death in December 2020, Maria admits it sparked a rollercoaster of emotions.

'I had one voicemail I'd unintentionally saved,' she remembers. 'I found it about a week after she died. It was a very mundane message asking me to put in a repeat prescription for her but it ended with "love you". It was like finding a tenner that you've forgotten about in a coat pocket.'

'I kept listening to it, just to hear her voice. Sometimes it made me smile. Other times I listened to it when I had a cry.

'It wasn't something I listened to on repeat for hours but perhaps once a day,' Maria adds. 'Then once every few days. Then it got to the point where I suppose I forgot about it, and now it's not there anymore, as my messages go after a set amount of time, and I'm ok with that.

'For those initial few weeks though, it was a real comfort.'

*8 January 2022*

# 10 things nobody tells you about losing a parent

Grief will vary from person to person, though there are certain emotions and circumstances that many of us will experience. It can often be a source of comfort to hear from someone who has experienced the emotional rollercoaster of losing a loved one and has come out on the other side. With this in mind, we present this guest post from Kiri Nowak, who blogs over at The Content Wolf. Kiri shares her experience of bereavement after losing a parent, and some things she's learned along the way.

It's hard to even put how it feels to lose a parent into words, but the key thing to keep in mind is there is no normal way of reacting. I haven't just felt one emotion since my father passed, my experience has been more like travelling the world. Each stage of your journey will be completely different, and as you wander through your grief, emotions will come and go.

It's been nearly 11 years since my father died (I was 18 when it happened), so I think I can safely say I've been through it all; the shock, the sadness, the anger, the guilt, and, eventually, the acceptance. There's no universal manual to help you deal with the loss of a parent, so when it does happen, a lot of feelings, occurrences and interactions with other people can take you by surprise.

From my personal experience, I've put together some things which I experienced that you might not have thought about or expected to happen. As soon as you lose a parent it feels like your life has fallen apart and you are caught up in a whirlwind, but you do eventually get your feet back on the ground, I promise. The pain doesn't go away, you just learn how to accept it, channel it and use it as a way of cherishing the person who was so cruelly taken from you.

## Here are ten things nobody tells you about losing a parent.

### It doesn't sink in for a while

Initially you might not feel anything. It may even seem like you are stuck in a dream, and everything that is going on isn't really happening. I definitely went through the first month, if not the first year on autopilot, but eventually everything does catch up with you and you start to feel less numb.

It's particularly hard when you lose a parent because initially you just can't face the prospect of living your life without them, and the only way for some people to cope is to pretend like it's not really happening. Confronting and accepting that the pain is there is scary, but you need to do it to start the grieving process.

### You don't have to be strong all the time

When my father died, I tried so hard to be strong for my mum and little sister, and show everybody how resilient and tough I was. But just remember you can only put on an act for so long. Pushing the pain below the surface so no one can see it is exhausting. It's OK to lose your composure, to have an outburst of emotion in public or privately at home or to completely fall apart. We take a lot of strength from our parents, so when you lose one of them, it's crushing.

30

## You will remember their best bits

One thing I've noticed is that you tend to idolise the parent you've lost. Why? Well, firstly, because they were your parent who you respected and loved, but also because you can't bear to criticise them in any way when they aren't around to defend themselves. It feels like the easiest way to remember them is in the best possible light. However, it's important to keep in mind not everyone's perfect, and it's OK to have negative memories as well as positive ones.

## You will probably feel guilty in some way, but you need to let it go

I've gone through the day my father died a thousand times and thought about what I could have done differently. I wasn't at home the last night he was alive, when he was in pain, for reasons I won't go into. This kills me. But I can't change it. I know if my dad was around he wouldn't hold it against me.

I've also gone back and punished myself mentally for all the times that I wasn't the perfect daughter, or when I was mean to my dad. My mum, sister and I used to gang up on him occasionally, because he was the only man in the house, but that's nothing unusual and he took it in his stride. It's not a reason for me to feel bad, because he knew exactly how much I loved him.

This isn't helpful, and you are just being unnecessarily cruel to yourself. Instead of focusing on what you didn't do or times where you messed up, remember the times you made your parent proud or happy.

## How lost you will feel

Your parents cared for you from the moment you entered this world, they nurtured you and showed you the way. So when you find yourself without one of your parents, you immediately feel lost. I think the hardest times for me have been when I've really needed to talk to my dad for advice.

When life has been tough, and I've needed his strength and his guidance, I've felt so lost and alone. But slowly I've learned to live with my father's spirit inside me, and if I'm completely honest, I usually know what he would say or want me to do even though he's not here to say it.

## Childhood memories fade faster than expected

My sister seems to have a much better memory than me, but one thing we both agree on is how hard it is to recall memories. It feels like he's slipping out my fingers, and as the years pass, the memories fade a little more. However, the important, wonderful, powerful memories never leave you, they stay with you forever.

Like the time when he cried when we made him a photo memory book for Christmas, when his voice boomed at me when he cheered me on at races, and when we sang Bruce Springsteen *Glory Days* until our lungs gave out on car journeys to Spain. Don't worry, even if you forget things over time, the best memories will never leave you.

## After a year or so, other people won't really care

People forget you are grieving. They offer their condolences in the first few weeks, sure, but not too long after that, they just get on with their lives, and it hurts. But don't take it to heart too much, it's just the way people are. It doesn't take away from what you are experiencing at all.

Just remember there are others going through the same as you, and they will be much more likely to understand. They will be the only people who truly, wholeheartedly get what you are going through.

For other people life goes on, which is cruel and thoughtless and it will no doubt make you angry. But it shouldn't, because they just don't understand. They haven't been through such a devastating loss. 11 years after my father's death I still suffer, but my close friends don't really see it. They can't relate to the fact that on some days, the pain I feel is still as raw as the day it happened.

## How painful important milestones are

When you lose a parent, it's the big milestones that really test you. The big birthdays, the achievements, the weddings and the thought of potentially having your own kids who will never know their grandad. However, there are ways to include your late parent in these milestones, and as time goes on, you see them as a chance to remember and celebrate their part in your life rather than simply suffering through these events all the time. For example, I'm getting married in eight months, and I've found some wonderfully touching and creative ways to make my father a part of the wedding, and these little things will no doubt help me get through the day and remember him with pride.

## How hard it is when you are unexpectedly reminded of your loss

Sometimes, you will be doing OK and managing your grief, when something catches you off guard. And then suddenly a surge of powerful emotion hits you like a tidal wave. For me I think the most challenging times have been when something has reminded me of my dad. When I watch a film and someone's dad dies, or when a song comes on the radio that reminds me of him, or most recently, when I was at a wedding and the bride unexpectedly called for a father daughter dance. Ouch. That hurts, especially as my wedding is coming up. But these moments, even though they are hard, sometimes they are the perfect way to let go of some of that emotion you've tried so hard to keep from bursting, and after you've had a little cry, you feel a little bit better.

## How you eventually come to view your grief with love and appreciation

I'm not going to lie, like I mentioned, at times, the pain is just as raw as it's ever been. But generally, I've entered a new stage of my grief. When I'm reminded of my dad, I use it as an opportunity to cherish his memory, and to dedicate a minute or two of my day to him, and someday, even if it doesn't feel like it, you will be able to do the same. Now I live every day and my father is there no matter what I'm doing, and I'm grateful he touched my life in such a powerful and beautiful way.

*8 September 2018*

# How different cultures view the end

By Sue Bryant

**D**eath is marked in so many ways around the world that an understanding of different rituals can be helpful, particularly in a cross cultural environment. It's not death, as such, which is a universal experience, but the expression of grief that differs so much between cultures.

## Death and dying: Korea

In Korea, where cremation is becoming commonplace nowadays, there is a trend to have the ashes of a loved one refined and turned into colourful beads. While these are not worn, if you visit a Korean home and see these beads on display, they're likely to be the ashes of a loved one of the homeowner.

## Death and dying: China

White is the colour of mourning in China, not black, as in the west, and as such, is regarded as unlucky; this is why giving white flowers to a Chinese person is inappropriate. Funeral rituals vary according to the age and status of the deceased but the official mourning period for a Buddhist may go on for 100 days. These rituals are elaborate and may even include hiring professional wailers, in the belief that the young in China no longer know how to show emotion appropriately. These mourners learn facts about the deceased and then start the process of expressing grief at the funeral, sobbing and wailing, opening the doors for any family mourners who feel embarrassed about public displays of emotion.

## Death and dying: Japan

Japan is the opposite. Death is seen as liberation and acceptance is more important than expressing oneself. People bring condolence money to wakes in white envelopes tied with black and white ribbon. Bodies are cremated but the ashes then separated from the bones, these remains sometimes being divided up between the temple, the family and even the employer of the departed. The dead are remembered during a three-day holiday in August, Obon, when the spirits of ancestors are believed to return to the family home, graves are cleaned and fires lit. This celebration of the dead is common in cultures where ancestor worship is practised. In these cultures, life is seen as cyclical rather than linear and the dead are believed to have powers over the living, such as the ability to bless or curse.

## Death and dying: Ghana

Ghana is another example of this belief in an afterlife, with a relatively new tradition of elaborate coffins, which will illustrate the interests, profession or status of the departed but also see them off into the next life in style. A coffin may take the form of an aeroplane, or a Porsche, or a Coca Cola bottle, an animal or even, in dubious taste, a giant cigarette packet. Coffin makers are highly sought after and are regarded as important artists. Funerals are enormous affairs, often costing more than weddings, and advertised on huge billboards so that nobody in the community misses out.

## Death and dying: Africa

In other parts of Africa, funeral rituals have evolved from the blending of Christian, Islam and traditional practices. In southern Africa, like Ghana, funerals are enormous affairs involving entire communities. The death is usually announced on the local radio station and mourners will gather over the coming days, coming from surrounding villages and further afield to pray and sing. As numbers swell, catering becomes more complex, with animals slaughtered to feed the crowd. If you are an employer in, say, Botswana or Namibia, you need to allow time off for funerals and if you employ several workers from the same community, you may well lose all of them for days at a time in the event of a death.

## Death and dying: Hindu faith

In the Hindu faith, it is preferable to die at home, surrounded by family. The soul is believed to go on, according to one's karma. Bodies are cremated quickly, usually within 24 hours, in order to liberate the soul quickly. Mourners wear white, not black, and people do not bring food to the wake, but to a ceremony 13 days after the cremation, at which the soul is liberated and the mourning period considered over. Ashes are scattered over water, the most desirable place being the holy Ganges, and a lot of Hindu families living outside India will make the pilgrimage to do this.

## Death and dying: Muslim faith

Muslims bury their dead, rather than cremate them, in the belief that there will be a physical resurrection on the Day of Judgment. The dead are buried facing Mecca and graves raised above the ground, or marked by stones, so nobody walks on them. Because the death of a Muslim is regarded as a loss to the Muslim community overall, it is not uncommon for people who did not even know the deceased to attend funerals. Crying is expected at burials but a loss of control, wailing and shrieking, is seen as inappropriate. A mourning period of up to 40 days follows a burial.

*2 February 2021*

# Five ways to honour a loved one's memory

We all grieve in different ways. For some people, looking through old photos brings comfort, for others seeing a reminder of their loved one brings the grief flooding back in.

**W**e've gathered together some ideas for how you might want to honour your loved one's memory. Some are tangible, constant reminders, others are reminders you can choose to visit in your own time, when you feel ready to do so. And some about actions you might want to take to honour them.

## 1. Dedicate a tree or woodland

Dedicating a tree or woodland is a living memorial to a loved one and dedications are available from a range of UK charities including in Woodland Trust woods across the UK and can range from individual trees to whole areas of woodland. When you make a dedication, you will receive a pack containing a certificate with a personal message, a map, and an information sheet to help you learn about the history and wildlife of your chosen wood – and how to visit.

The National Trust has an ambition to plant 20 million trees by 2030. You can make a dedication via their website to celebrate a loved one's life while also giving back to nature.

If you'd prefer to plant a tree in your garden or on land you own, check the best time of year to plant the type of tree you have chosen. Bare-rooted trees are best planted between November and March. The Woodland Trust's website has advice on how to plant native woodland trees and fruit trees in the UK.

## 2. Make a memory bear

Memory bears are made with clothing that belonged to a loved one or material that has some sentimental meaning for you. They give you something tangible that you can hold for comfort as well as incorporating visual reminders. Memory bears are often made to give to younger family memories as a keepsake.

A favourite jumper, jeans, rugby shirt, or part of a wedding dress can be incorporated into a cushion or bear. You can buy a pattern and make your own or, if you prefer to have your keepsake made for you, there are many suppliers on Etsy.

## 3. Design a piece of memorial jewellery

Memorial jewellery is a keepsake which contains the ashes of someone who's been cremated. There are various types available, suitable for different budgets.  Because of its unparalleled beauty, durability, and uniqueness, many people choose to have memorial jewellery made from diamonds.

Only a small amount of ash is needed to create a piece of memorial jewellery. This gives you the freedom to divide the ashes up between family members. Designing a one-of-a-kind piece of jewellery gives you an opportunity to reflect on your loved one and reminisce about your time together.

Every time you see your ring, pendant, earrings, or cufflinks, you'll be reminded of your loved one and the happy times you spent together. Your personal keepsake can also act as a reminder of the fragility of life and the importance of living every day to its full potential.

Diamonds made from ashes and mined diamonds are identical, both chemically and aesthetically. The only difference in their creation is that mined diamonds are made from applying high pressure and high temperature naturally, while memorial diamonds are made by applying high pressure and high temperatures inside a lab.

## 4. Make a donation to their favourite charity

You can honour someone's beliefs and interests by making a donation to their favourite charity.

## 5. Live your best life

The old adage 'Life's too short' can sometimes hit home when someone you love dies. It can make you assess your own life and clarify for you changes you want to make. As a result, some people choose to honour the memory of a loved one by changing something about their own lives: to give their life purpose, to slow down, to travel,  or to strive for happiness.

Humanists believe we have only one life and so we should make the most of it. For us, being happy is one of the most important things in life. But we don't think of our own happiness in isolation: we take into account the health and wellbeing of others, and the care and protection of the environment.

Many humanists believe that building positive relationships, finding peace and tranquillity, and pursuing intellectual endeavours are all important ingredients of 'the good life' and can make us happy.

**'The happy life is to an extraordinary extent the same as the good life.' Bertrand Russell (1872 – 1970)**

The humanist goal is for everyone to be happy and recognise that our own happiness is tied up with everyone else's.

**'Happiness is the only good. The place to be happy is here. The time to be happy is now. The way to be happy is to make others so.' Robert Ingersoll, 'The Great Agnostic' (1833 – 1899)**

# Britons on their funeral and how long they think they will be remembered for

An extract from the YouGov Death Study.

## How many Britons have thought about their funeral?

Half of Britons (49%) say they have pictured what their funeral will look like, the YouGov Death Study finds.

Four in ten (41%) have thought about it in general, while 8% have looked at it in detail. Half (48%), however, have not given any thought to this.

Notably more British women (55%) than men (42%) say they have thought about their funeral arrangements, and this applies across all age groups.

Among the older population, over half (55%) of those aged 60+ have considered what their funeral will look like, which is higher than in the younger age groups. Older women (60 or above) are twice as likely (12%) as men of the same age (5%) to report thinking in detail about their funeral arrangements.

## What do Britons want to happen to their body when they die?

Just 15% of Britons say they'd like to be buried. The greatest number – just under half (45%) – want to be cremated, with this view being expressed by slightly more women (48%) than men (42%).

The older Britons are, the more likely they are to say they'd like their body to be cremated, with this preference growing from 22% among 16-24-year-olds, to 58% among those who are 60 or older.

Among the one in five Britons who are religious and actively practising their faith, a similar number want to be buried (34%) as cremated (36%). For those who are religious but don't practise, 54% prefer to be cremated, compared to 16% who prefer burial. For Britons who do not belong to any religious denomination, 8% would like to be buried and 45% would like to be cremated.

The data also shows that one in eight Britons (13%) say they'd like to donate their body for research. This applies to 18% of those who say they don't belong to any faith, which is three times higher compared to those who practise their religion (6%).

## How many Britons expect to be remembered when they're gone?

The YouGov Death Study also researched for how long Britons think they will be remembered following their death.

A quarter (24%) think people will remember them for five (15%) or ten (9%) years after they die. One in eight (13%) think they will be remembered for up to 20 years, and 11% expect the memory of them will live on for half a century after they're gone.

Just 7% think they will be remembered for longer than 50 years. Young Britons (16-24) are twice as likely than other age groups to say they expect to be remembered for longer than 50 years: 13% vs 5-6% of those 25 and above. This view is most notably present among 16-24 year old men (19%), who are more likely than their female peers (8%) to expect to be remembered longer than half a century.

On the other end are the 9% of Britons who expect to not be remembered at all. For those who are in their 60s or older, more men (11%) than women (6%) think they won't be remembered at all following their death.

*6 October 2021*

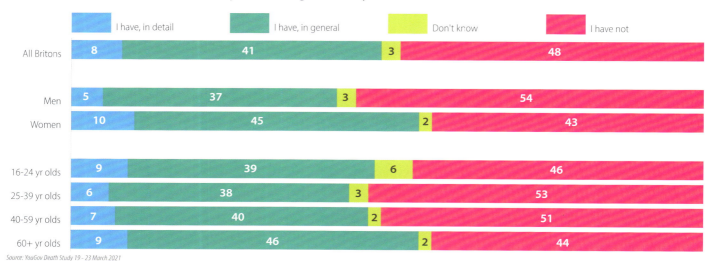

## Around half of Britons have imagined what their funeral will look like

Have you ever imagined what your funeral will look like? %

| | I have, in detail | I have, in general | Don't know | I have not |
|---|---|---|---|---|
| All Britons | 8 | 41 | 3 | 48 |
| Men | 5 | 37 | 3 | 54 |
| Women | 10 | 45 | 2 | 43 |
| 16-24 yr olds | 9 | 39 | 6 | 46 |
| 25-39 yr olds | 6 | 38 | 3 | 53 |
| 40-59 yr olds | 7 | 40 | 2 | 51 |
| 60+ yr olds | 9 | 46 | 2 | 44 |

*Source: YouGov Death Study 19 - 23 March 2021*

## Older Britons want to be cremated when they die, younger people are less certain

What would you like to happen to your body when you die? %

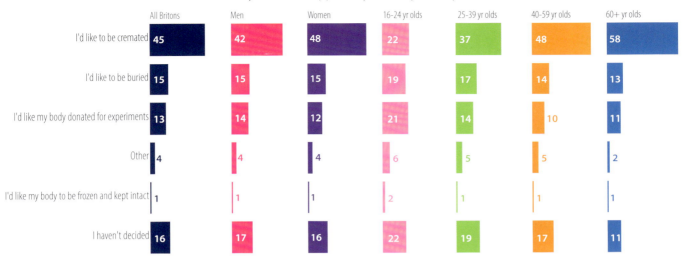

| | All Britons | Men | Women | 16-24 yr olds | 25-39 yr olds | 40-59 yr olds | 60+ yr olds |
|---|---|---|---|---|---|---|---|
| I'd like to be cremated | 45 | 42 | 48 | 22 | 37 | 48 | 58 |
| I'd like to be buried | 15 | 15 | 15 | 19 | 17 | 14 | 13 |
| I'd like my body donated for experiments | 13 | 14 | 12 | 21 | 14 | 10 | 11 |
| Other | 4 | 4 | 4 | 6 | 5 | 5 | 2 |
| I'd like my body to be frozen and kept intact | 1 | 1 | 1 | 2 | 1 | 1 | 1 |
| I haven't decided | 16 | 17 | 16 | 22 | 19 | 17 | 11 |

*Source: YouGov Death Study 19 - 23 March 2021*

## Britons who are not religious are much more likely to say they want their body donated for experiments when they die

What would you like to happen to your body when you die? %

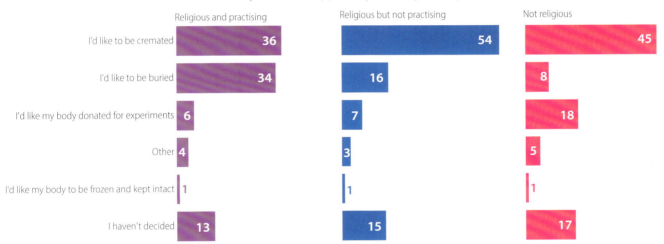

| | Religious and practising | Religious but not practising | Not religious |
|---|---|---|---|
| I'd like to be cremated | 36 | 54 | 45 |
| I'd like to be buried | 34 | 16 | 8 |
| I'd like my body donated for experiments | 6 | 7 | 18 |
| Other | 4 | 3 | 5 |
| I'd like my body to be frozen and kept intact | 1 | 1 | 1 |
| I haven't decided | 13 | 15 | 17 |

*Source: YouGov Death Study 19 - 23 March 2021*

## A third of Britons expect to be remembered for ten years at most after they die

How long do you think people will remember you after you die? %

| | All Britons | Men | Women | 16-24 yr olds | 25-39 yr olds | 40-59 yr olds | 60+ yr olds |
|---|---|---|---|---|---|---|---|
| Not at all | 9 | 10 | 8 | 7 | 8 | 10 | 8 |
| Up to five years | 15 | 16 | 13 | 14 | 16 | 15 | 14 |
| Up to ten years | 9 | 9 | 10 | 10 | 9 | 11 | 8 |
| Up to twenty years | 13 | 12 | 12 | 11 | 11 | 12 | 15 |
| Up to fifty years | 11 | 11 | 11 | 7 | 9 | 12 | 15 |
| Longer than fifty years | 7 | 7 | 7 | 13 | 6 | 5 | 6 |

*Source: YouGov Death Study 19 - 23 March 2021*

# How to be a 'grief ally'

You might have found yourself here as someone you love has experienced the death of someone special to them. You may be thinking, 'what is a grief ally and how can I be one?'. A 'grief ally' is simply someone who wants to show up and be present for their person who is grieving, in whatever way is helpful to them. There are many ways in which you can support a bereaved person, check out our tips below:

## 1. Show up no matter what

Be present with your loved one. Show them that you care about how they are feeling and that you want to support them through their bereavement. Its normal to feel worried or anxious about supporting a bereaved young person. Sometimes, this worry can lead to avoiding the topic of loss or the person altogether through fear of saying the 'wrong thing'. The wrong thing would be complete avoidance - this can be really upsetting for the bereaved young person as it can leave them feeling isolated in their grief. The most important thing you can do for a bereaved young person is offer your time and presence. If you don't know what to say, just sit with them and listen - knowing they can rely on you can be the most healing gift you can give to them.

## 2. Offer to practically support them

Losing a loved one is a world-changing experience. A bereaved young person's life will now look very different from before. They may not be able to or want to do the things which were part of their usual routine. It can be unhelpful to say to a bereaved young person, 'let me know if you need anything' - the likelihood is that they won't reach out and ask. Instead, offer to practically help with things such as driving them to or going with them to an appointment or organising a specific day/time to go out for lunch or a walk together. You will know the bereaved young person best, it's important to think what could you practically do to support them best.

## 3. Understand that grief doesn't 'go away'

The truth is that grief is never ending. It is not a task to be completed and there is no time-line for the bereaved young person to follow. Therefore, the bereaved young person will be grieving for the rest of their lives. As a grief ally, it is important to understand this and to be aware that the bereaved young person will continue to share memories or emotions regarding the loss of their loved one as time passes. A misconception of grief is that it is only felt for a short time after someone dies, so don't be alarmed if the bereaved young person is still grieving weeks, months or years down the line - this is completely normal.

## 4. Note important dates

Set reminders on your phone or jot them down on a calendar of important dates for the bereaved young person. This could be days such as anniversaries, birthdays, Father's Day, Mother's Day etc. By remembering these days, it means you can reach out to them to show your solidarity as a grief ally, to show them that you care about them on that difficult day. You could simply send them a text or make plans to spend time with them if that is what they would like. It is important to understand that grief is individual to each person. One bereaved young person may find comfort in being surrounded by people on a difficult day, whilst others might like to spend the day alone. The best way to find out what is most supportive for the bereaved young person is to simply ask them what works for them.

## 5. Respect their reality

Listen and truly respect the bereaved young person's reality. When we are outside of a situation, it can be difficult to understand where someone is coming from or how they are actually feeling. Sometimes, we tend to make situations seem less bad than they actually are as a way of providing comfort to the individual. However, as a grief ally, it is important to note that you can never 'fix' the bereaved young person's grief. The best thing you can do is to validate their grief by saying things such as 'I'm sorry you are going through this right now, I wish I could make it better but know that I am going to be with you every step of your grief journey'.

## 6. Talk about their loved one

It is common to feel anxious about talking about the bereaved young person's loved one through fear of upset. However, the reality is that the worst has already happened - there isn't much you could say to cause more pain or upset. Therefore, choosing to talk about the bereaved young person's loved one is actually a really empowering and caring thing to do. This shows the bereaved young person that you haven't forgotten about their loved one and that you will actively help the bereaved young person to carry their loved one's legacy with them on their grief journey.

## 7. Be understanding of what grief looks like to them

Respect that grief is individual and that some say it is as unique as a snow-flake. Therefore, try to understand how grief may look and feel for the bereaved young person. This may mean that the ways in which they choose to cope may be different to how you might grieve and that is ok. As long as the bereaved young person is not taking part in any self-destructive or self-harming behaviours, it is important to respect and support them fully in how they choose to grieve. If the bereaved young person is showing self-destructive or self-harming behaviours, it is vital to get

them the appropriate help. Childline share information on self-harm, suicidal thoughts and how to help a friend going through these things.

## 8. Suggest support services

Experiencing grief after the death of a loved one is a normal response. Many bereaved people may only need support from those closest to them. However, some may need or want support outside of their usual support circle and that is ok. If you or the bereaved person feels they may need extra support, you can encourage them to give it a go. Tell the bereaved young person about our Hope Again website and the resources we share to offer support through grief. You can also encourage them to send an email to us anytime at: hopeagain@cruse.org.uk. If the bereaved young person would like on-going, practical support - they can receive this through Cruse Bereavement Support. The support can be offered in the form of face-to-face sessions, online or via the helpline. To find out more, call the free helpline on: 0808 808 1677.

## 9. Look after yourself

Be aware that being a grief ally can be a very overwhelming and tiring experience. Therefore, it is important to take time out to re-charge from supporting the bereaved young person. Remember, you are doing the best you can and you are showing up because you care - your support doesn't go unnoticed and it will have a positive and lasting effect on the bereaved young person's grief journey. Truthfully, you never know when you may need someone to be a grief ally for you so be the grief ally you may need someday.

**www.hopeagain.org.uk**

# What to say to someone who has been bereaved

When someone dies, it can be hard to know what to say to those who were close to them. While each bereaved person's experience will be different, these tips will give you ideas for how to help them feel heard and supported through their grief.

## Things that can be helpful

### Say how sorry you are

When someone is grieving, it's important to acknowledge what has happened and express your sympathy. This can be as brief as saying 'I'm so sorry for your loss', or 'I heard about your dad, I'm so sorry'.

### Share a memory

If you knew the person who has died, you could also share a memory or say what they meant to you. You might say something like, 'I remember your mum's brilliant speech at your wedding', or 'I'll miss your grandad's wonderful sense of humour'.

### Offer them space to talk

Many bereaved people say it helps to be able to speak freely about how they're feeling. Saying 'how are you doing?' gives them a chance to talk about it if they want to.

If you know the person quite well, you could ask them directly, 'Would you like to talk about it?'. Let them know you're happy to listen to any feelings they want to share.

### Tell them however they feel is OK

People who are grieving can experience a huge range of emotions, including shock, sadness, pain, anger, guilt, anxiety and numbness. Their feelings will be unique to them and their relationship with the person who has died.

If they do talk to you about their grief, be open to whatever emotions they are experiencing. Let them know that however they feel is OK – there is no 'right' way to grieve.

### Recognise how hard it is for them

When someone is going through a bereavement, you may want to take their pain away.

Although this isn't possible, acknowledging it by saying, 'I'm sorry I can't make things better', 'I'm sorry it's so hard for you', or 'I'm sorry things are so tough right now' can help them feel heard and supported.

### Ask if there is anything they need

You may want to help but not know how. Ask the bereaved person if there is anything they need, and let them know you're ready to support them. If they seem unsure, you could suggest specific things, such as cooking them a meal or doing their shopping.

### Tell them you're thinking of them

Sending someone who is grieving a message to say you're thinking of them will show them they don't have to cope alone. You may not be able to change what they are going through, but knowing you care could give them some comfort.

### Sometimes you don't need to say anything

When you are with a bereaved person, take your cue from them in terms of how much they want to talk. It may be that just spending time quietly alongside someone can help them cope with their grief.

## Things to avoid saying

### Don't make assumptions about how they feel

You may have experienced a loss in the past and feel you understand what someone is going through, but everyone experiences grief differently. Give the bereaved person the space to tell you how they are feeling, and avoid saying things like, 'You must be feeling...' or 'I know exactly how you feel'.

### Avoid trying to fix things

It can be tempting to try and make someone who is grieving feel better. That's why, if someone has died after a long illness, people might say things like, 'It was for the best', or 'She's at peace now'. When someone dies in old age, they may say, 'At least he had a long life'.

Statements like these aren't always helpful. The bereaved person might not feel the same way or may not find it comforting, and they could resent being told what to think.

### Don't tell them they will 'heal', 'move on' or 'get over it'

When someone is first bereaved, they may not be able to imagine a future without the person who has died. They might worry about their memories fading, and find the idea of 'moving on' or 'getting over it' very upsetting. People often say 'time is a healer', but bereavement isn't about healing so much as finding ways to live with grief.

### Avoid setting expectations around how long grief will last

Most people find ways to cope with their grief and feel better over time. But setting a specific timeframe (for example, by saying something like, 'It took my uncle two years to recover after my aunt died') can make them feel they are failing if things don't improve. In reality, the grieving process is different for everyone and it can take years.

### Be careful talking about religious ideas

After someone dies, people sometimes say things like, 'He's in a better place now', or 'It was God's will'. But a bereaved person may not believe in God, or may not agree. If they do believe, they may even feel God has taken their loved one, and be angry. When it comes to religion, be guided by things the bereaved person says and only mention it if it feels appropriate.

The above information is reprinted with kind permission from Sue Ryder.
© 2022 Sue Ryder

www.sueryder.org

# Where can I find help?

Below are some telephone numbers, email addresses and websites of agencies or charities that can offer support or advice if you or someone you know needs it.

**At a Loss**
Website: ataloss.org
AtaLoss provides the UK's bereavement signposting website- www.ataloss.org. Most UK bereavement services are listed, along with helplines, useful books and pages of practical advice. Also find a free counselling web-chat service. Everything you need in one place and easy to use.

**Blue Cross – Pet Bereavement Support**
Helpline: 0800 096 6606

**Child Bereavement UK**
Helpline: 0800 02 888 40
Website: childbereavement.org.uk

**The Compassionate Friends**
Helpline: 0345 123 2304
Website: tcf.org.uk

**Cruse Bereavement Care**
Day by Day Helpline: 0808 808 1677
Website: cruse.org.uk

**Cruse Scotland**
Helpline: 0808 802 6161
Website: crusescotland.org.uk

**The Good Grief Trust**
Website: thegoodgrieftrust.org

**Grief Encounter**
Grieftalk Helpline: 0808 802 0111
(9am-9pm Mon-Fri)
Website: griefencounter.org.uk

**Hope Again**
Website: hopeagain.org.uk

**Marie Curie**
Bereavement Support Helpline:
0800 090 2309
Website: mariecurie.org.uk

**SOBS - Survivors of Bereavement by Suicide**
Helpline: 0300 111 5065
Website: uk-sobs.org.uk

**Sudden**
Helpline: 0800 2600 400
Website: sudden.org

**Way Widowed & Young**
Website: widowedandyoung.org.uk
WAY offers support to widowed men and women up to the age of 50, parents and those without children.

**Winston's Wish**
Helpline: 08088 020 021
Website: winstonswish.org
Winston's Wish supports children and young people to rebuild their life after a family bereavement.

# Key Facts

- Brain waves, called alpha and gamma, change pattern even after blood stops flowing to the brain. (page 5)

- If humans can be resuscitated after six, seven, eight or even ten minutes in extreme cases, it could theoretically be hours before their brain shuts down completely. (page 5)

- 9% of Britons report thinking about death – either their own or in general – at least once a day. (page 6)

- Britons aged 16-24 are twice as likely (12%) than those 60 or older (6%) to report thinking about death on a daily basis, with 25-59 year olds sitting in between at 10%. (page 6)

- Two-thirds (65%) of Britons think there are things that are worse than dying. (page 6)

- When asked how the death of someone has impacted them, the most common response, at 38%, was that Britons began to appreciate life more itself, with this view being shared more by women (40%) than men (35%). (page 7)

- More women (31%) than men (21%) say that somebody's death made them stronger. (page 7)

- 49 per cent of people do not have a will. (page 10)

- People living together without being married or a civil partnership, have no legal right to any assets. (page 10)

- You can legally write a will from the age of 18. (page 11)

- The average 'cost of dying' is now at £9,263 in the UK. (page 13)

- The cost of dying has risen 39 per cent in the last decade. (page 13)

- The average cost of a basic funeral which includes cremation or burial, and the fees for a doctor, funeral director, and a minister or celebrant, was £4,184 in 2020. (page 14)

- More than a third of families have no savings for the cost of a funeral. (page 14)

- 17 per cent of people waited more than three months before they could close a loved one's bank account. (page 15)

- The time spent in a period of bereavement will be different for everybody and depends on factors such as the type of relationship, the strength of attachment or intimacy to the person who died, the situation surrounding their death, and the amount of time spent anticipating the death. (page 16)

- The five stages of grief model was developed by Elisabeth Kübler-Ross, and became famous after she published her book On Death and Dying in 1969. (page 21)

- Research estimates that 8,000 Facebook users died daily in 2018. (page 27)

- White is the colour of mourning in China, not black. (page 32)

- Half of Britons (49%) say they have pictured what their funeral will look like. (page 34)

- Just 15% of Britons say they'd like to be buried. (page 34)

- The older Britons are, the more likely they are to say they'd like their body to be cremated, with this preference growing from 22% among 16-24-year-olds, to 58% among those who are 60 or older. (page 34)

- 9% of Britons expect to not be remembered at all after they die. (page 34)

## Bereavement

To experience a loss; the loss of a loved one through their death.

## Cemetery/graveyard

Area of land where bodies are buried (unless cremated) and headstones erected to remember the dead. It is usually found attached to a place of worship or crematorium.

## Coroner

A doctor or lawyer responsible for investigating deaths.

## Cremation

A method of disposing of a dead body by burning. The ashes produced are given to the family of the deceased, who can either keep them or choose to scatter them, often in a favourite place of the deceased.

## Death Cafe

A fairly recent idea, a Death Cafe where a group can discuss death, drink tea and eat cake. It is generally a group-directed discussion of death with no agenda, objectives or themes. It is a discussion group rather than a grief support or counselling session, although people grieving may find them helpful.

## Digital legacy

It is not clear what should happen to a person's online data when they die. This includes all their online accounts, such as e-mail, banking and social networking sites. This can also have an effect on their digital assets, such as music, films and even computer game characters - who has the right to decide what will be done with them? Should family members be allowed to have access to them?

## Eco/green funeral

People are now environmentally aware and are now opting for 'eco' funerals. This means that people are planning 'green' funerals that will have a minimal impact on the environment, such as a woodland funeral on an eco site. This can involve a coffin that is biodegradable (e.g. cardboard or willow), no embalming or toxic chemicals are to be used on the body or the coffin and often a tree is planted in place of a headstone.

## Eulogy

A speech delivered at a funeral, praising the person who has died and reminiscing about their life.

## Executor

Someone responsible for the administration of a person's estate after their death, usually nominated by the deceased in their will.

## Funeral

A ceremony, often faith-based and held in a place of worship, which friends and family of the deceased can attend as a way of saying goodbye to their loved one.

## Funeral poverty

Funerals can be expensive: according to the University of Bath's Institute for Policy Research, the average cost of a funeral and burial or cremation is now around £3,500. With the growing costs of dying, people simply cannot afford to pay for a funeral - they quite literally 'cannot afford to die'.

## Grief

An intense feeling of sorrow felt after a bereavement; the process of facing the loss of someone you love.

## Headstone

Also known as a tombstone or gravestone. A stone monument erected to a dead person, usually inscribed with their name and dates of birth and death, which friends and family can visit as a way of remembering the dead person. It is usually found in a cemetery.

## Living funeral

An end of life celebration arranged while the person, who is most probably suffering from a terminal illness or has a sense that their time is short, is still alive.

## Mourning/grieving

A period during which an individual is in a state of grief. The phrase 'to be in mourning' is more specific - it suggests the observation of certain conventions, for example wearing black.

## Post-mortem

A medical procedure carried out on a dead body to discover the cause of death where this is unclear.

## Terminal illness

An illness for which there is no cure and which will ultimately bring about the patient's death.

## Undertaker

Also known as the funeral director. A person who is responsible for organising funerals and preparing bodies for burial or cremation.

## Widow/Widower

A widow is a woman whose husband has died. A man whose wife has died is called a widower.

## Will

A will, also known as a Last Will and Testament, is a legal document that spells out your wishes for your money, property and possessions after you die. It can also appoint guardians for any children.

# Activities

## Brainstorming

♦ As a class, discuss what you understand about death and bereavement:

- What is bereavement?
- What is grief?
- What is a widow?
- What is a widower?
- What is a funeral?
- What is a will?
- What are digital assets?

## Research

♦ Do some research into the types of funerals on offer in the UK and look at the costs involved in different areas of the country. Prepare a graph to show your findings.

♦ Prepare a questionnaire for your family and friends. Have they considered what type of funeral they would prefer? Do they have a favourite song they would like played? You should ask at least seven questions. Write some notes on your findings and share with the rest of your class.

♦ In pairs, choose a country other than your own. Do some research into funeral practices in that country. Create a poster to show some facts about the funeral practices.

♦ In pairs, do some research into what happens to social media accounts when someone dies. Write a report and feedback to your class.

♦ Do some research into digital assets. What are digital assets? You should consider the different types of digital assets people have and how these might be accessed after their death.

## Design

♦ Design a poster with some of the signs of grief and tips to help overcome these.

♦ In small groups, design an app which will allow students to gain confidential advice about how to deal with grief.

♦ Design a signposting poster with charities and organisations that offer bereavement support.

♦ Create a leaflet with tips on how to offer support to someone who has been bereaved.

♦ Choose an article from this book and create an illustration for it.

## Oral

♦ In small groups, discuss the issue of taking children to funerals. What age do you think it might be appropriate for them to attend? How do you think a child could be prepared for this event?

♦ Divide the class in half. Debate burials versus cremations. One group should argue for burials and the other for cremations.

♦ Choose one of the illustrations in this book and, with a partner, discuss why the artist chose to portray the article in the way they did.

♦ In small groups, discuss why making a will is a good idea. What sort of things should be included and why?

## Reading/writing

♦ Imagine you are an Agony Aunt/Uncle. A teen has written to you saying that they are struggling after a recent death. Write a suitable reply and let them know what help is available.

♦ Write an article for your school/college newspaper explaining why it's important to seek help if you are suffering from grief and find you cannot cope with your feelings. Include some information about organisations that can help.

♦ Write an article exploring how the Internet is changing the way in which people grieve.

♦ Read The Fault in Our Stars by John Green. Write a review.

♦ Read Funeral Blues by W.H. Auden. Write down how this poem made you feel, which parts stood out to you as describing the feeling of grief?

♦ Write your own poem about grief, use Funeral Blues by W.H. Auden and Do Not Go Gentle Into That Good Night by Dylan Thomas for inspiration.

# Acknowledgements

The publisher is grateful for permission to reproduce the material in this book. While every care has been taken to trace and acknowledge copyright, the publisher tenders its apology for any accidental infringement or where copyright has proved untraceable. The publisher would be pleased to come to a suitable arrangement in any such case with the rightful owner.

The material reproduced in **issues** books is provided as an educational resource only. The views, opinions and information contained within reprinted material in **issues** books do not necessarily represent those of Independence Educational Publishers and its employees.

## Images

Cover image courtesy of iStock. All other images courtesy Freepik, Pixabay & Unsplash.

## Illustrations

Simon Kneebone: pages 23,24 & 36. Angelo Madrid: pages 12, 17 & 30.

## Additional acknowledgements

With thanks to the Independence team: Shelley Baldry, Tracy Biram and Jackie Staines.

Danielle Lobban

Cambridge, January 2022